DB

6-27-11

Parenting and Teaching the Gifted

Second Edition

Rosemary Callard-Szulgit

ROWMAN & LITTLEFIELD EDUCATION
A division of
ROWMAN & LITTLEFIELD PUBLISHERS, INC.
Lanham • New York • Toronto • Plymouth, UK

Published by Rowman & Littlefield Education
A division of Rowman & Littlefield Publishers, Inc.
A wholly owned subsidiary of The Rowman & Littlefield Publishing Group, Inc.
4501 Forbes Boulevard, Suite 200, Lanham, Maryland 20706
http://www.rowmaneducation.com

Estover Road, Plymouth PL6 7PY, United Kingdom

British Library Cataloguing in Publication Information Available

Library of Congress Cataloging-in-Publication Data

Callard-Szulgit, Rosemary, 1946-
  Parenting and teaching the gifted / Rosemary Callard-Szulgit. — 2nd ed.
    p. cm.
  Includes bibliographical references and index.
  ISBN 978-1-60709-455-5 (cloth : alk. paper) — ISBN 978-1-60709-457-9 (electronic)
  1. Gifted children—Education. 2. Education—Parent participation. I. Title.
  LC3993.2.C35 2010
  371.95–dc22

                                                                    2010008204

♾ ™ The paper used in this publication meets the minimum requirements of American
National Standard for Information Sciences—Permanence of Paper for Printed Library
Materials, ANSI/NISO Z39.48-1992.

Printed in the United States of America

Contents

Preface

Writing this book has been a pleasure for me as a practical part of my forty-two-year career in the public school and university settings; settings in which education for the gifted has been accepted/ignored, exemplified/denounced, and touted as elitist/integrated for all ability students. I have been able to help hundreds, if not thousands, of students and their parents understand and benefit from the strategies and programs available for gifted children, which work for all children. I've also helped dispel many of the *myths* associated with gifted children.

We know that differentiation is beneficial for all students—that higher-level thinking skills are essential for everyone.

Synthesis, or creativity, is a joyful key in the learning process. Students thrive when making learning their own, displaying application projects with their very own creative touch.

Compacting can save weeks, months, and even years of repetitive work for gifted children.

Using an inclusive process, rather than an exclusive program, has become a much more healthy way to assimilate the education for our cognitively gifted children in today's schools—avoiding the labels of "you're gifted, you're not; you're in, you're out!" The dividing lines between the supposed "haves" and "have nots" are continuing to be erased.

Yes, I do believe all children are gifted with individual and unique traits of their very own! However, we do have a cadre of children whose cognitive abilities far surpass those of their peers. Their knowledge base is far more expansive. To have these students study grade-level curricular areas they've already mastered year after year after year is unacceptable.

All children deserve to be educated at their levels of aptitude and accomplishment. *All*!

Teachers cannot do it alone. As the school day demands increased responsibilities in our ever-changing society, educators are desperately trying to service children with a multitude of thinking levels and emotional development in their classrooms. Parents can help. Administrators can help. District staff development coordinators can help by providing education in understanding the gifted and providing trainers in our school districts.

As a recovering perfectionist, I understand well the emotional pain that accompanies this dilemma for so many of our gifted children—their parents, too. We can provide counseling and many fine self-help books for these children to read and talk through with us.

Study skills and procrastination are not unique to just one or two achievement levels of children. Gifted children also need help in these arenas. Time management continues to be a necessity for our multipotential students, their parents, and other family members.

We can all help make this world a little better place, as we help one another foster excellence and applicability in our schools throughout the country.

Writing this book and supporting parents and teachers of gifted children as they realize the best education for their children is my way of helping make this world a little better place in my lifetime.

Read, enjoy, and know I admire every single one of you parents and educators who are giving your best to this country's children—all of them. I am trying to do the same.

Your friend and educator,
Rosemary S. Callard-Szulgit, Ed.D.

Acknowledgments

First and foremost, I'd like to thank my husband, Karl, whose brilliance and magnanimous caring of family and friends I truly honored and admired.

I thank my mom, Josephine Stiles Callard, a women decades ahead of her time—with profound intelligence, beautiful, very much a lady, and always giving of herself to others, through life, church, family, and community.

Thanks to my dad, Chesbro Callard, whose intelligence I admired and whose down-to-earth approach helped keep me grounded.

I honor my friends and say "thank you" for always loving and supporting me—Jeanette, Virginia, Carolyn, Shelly, Greg, Mark, Eric, and Fern.

And thanks to Brenda, for typing and tech support. You truly are a sweetheart! Thank you.

Introduction

Since writing the first edition of this book in 2003, I have happily seen a raising of the bar in educating our students—all students—gifted, twice-exceptional, underachieving, and the norm. Much of this has come about as a result of the emphasis on curriculum differentiation, spearheaded by Carol Tomlinson.

That's the good news. The sad news is that literally hundreds and thousands of our nation's education colleges are still graduating teachers with no background coursework in the needs, characteristics, and identification of academically gifted children. I simply do not understand how this can be, knowing that what works for gifted works for all children. However, let's continue to focus on the good news.

We now better understand the gifted, psychologically, as Michael Piechowski (2006) delineates the five dimensions of the psychological lives, as originated by Kazimierz Daprowski: psychomotor, sensual, intellectual, imaginational, and emotional.

We know asynchronous development is a common characteristic found in gifted children, where one area of a child's development progresses at a faster pace than another. We don't expect these children to perform perfectly in all areas at all times. However, many gifted children do expect themselves to always be perfect, and if one of their academic or physical skills is not as exemplary as all their others, they sometimes view themselves as failures. Perfectionism can and does cause personal pain, social adjustment problems, depression, angst, and underachievement in many of today's gifted children. Hess (1994, 29) defines perfectionism as the pursuit of excellence taken to the extreme. Perfectionists can create and not feel comfortable knowing when to stop. They often fear failure and avoid new experiences. They have exceedingly high expectations for themselves and others. Thankfully, books, articles, educators, and counselors are in fine tune now with perfectionism and how it affects our gifted, citing ways to better help these children and their parents.

Sisk (2009) has reminded us that peace begins with the individual, and mindfulness, compassion, loving kindness, consciousness, and mediation all lend a sense of peace and tranquility to our children.

In the past, parents of gifted children have often experienced the frustration of trying to get an appropriate education for their children in public and private schools.

Teachers of gifted have equally experienced the frustration of trying to educate their gifted students while the requirements of special education, the inclusion model, blending, and other classroom demands increasingly fragment their time and energies in a world that can be overwhelming.

We have been and are now making progress in the ever-expanding world of gifted children and their education/socialization. The information on parenting and teaching the gifted is presented through six main chapters. The format is question and answer, aimed at helping parents, teachers, and children find solutions to their queries through time-tested applicable solutions. Parents, teachers, and students alike, I salute you. We're all here to help each other. I offer this book as my way of helping. I wish you well.

Chapter One

Who Are the Gifted and Talented?

Q. What exactly does being "gifted" mean?

A. By definition, the U.S. Department of Education reflects today's knowledge and thinking about gifted children (Ross, 1993, 26):

> Children and youth with outstanding talent who perform or show the potential for performing at remarkably high levels of accomplishment when compared with others of their age, experience or environment.
>
> These children and youth exhibit high performance capability in intellectual, creative, and/or artistic areas, possess an unusual leadership capacity, or excel in specific academic fields. They require services or activities not ordinarily provided by the school.
>
> Outstanding talents are present in children and youth from all cultural groups, across all economic strata, and in all areas of human endeavor.

Whether you choose to support the use of this definition or not, the fact remains that there are hundreds and thousands of children in our schools whose thinking and comprehension abilities far surpass the norm of their peers.

Howard Gardner (1999) has helped expand our understanding of human intelligence and gifts with his theory of the nine multiple intelligences, as follows:

- Linguistic Intelligence—the capacity to use language to express what's on your mind and to understand other people.
- Logical/Mathematical Intelligence—The capacity to understand the underlying principle of some kind of casual system, the way a scientist or a logician does.

- Musical Rhythmic Intelligence—the capacity to think in music.
- Bodily/Kinesthetic Intelligence—the capacity to use your whole body or parts of your body to solve a problem.
- Spatial Intelligence—the ability to represent the spatial world internally in your mind.
- Naturalist Intelligence—the ability to discriminate among living things such as plants and animals and sensitivity to other features of the natural world.
- Intrapersonal Intelligence—having an understanding of yourself.
- Interpersonal Intelligence—the ability to understand other people.
- Existential Intelligence—the ability and proclivity to pose and ponder questions about life, death, and ultimate realities.

During the last two decades of the twentieth century, many of our schools' gifted programs focused more on the verbal/linguistics and logical/mathematical aspects of intelligence. Gifted education in the twenty-first century is much more in tune with servicing the wealth of "gifts" and "learning styles" we've learned about through ongoing research and best practices.

Q. I live in a small suburban school district that does not have a positive or proactive stance toward gifted children. In fact, each year that I've met with my nine-year-old's teachers, they have continued to say, "Clyde doesn't need any extra help. He's achieving As and doing well." I know he is becoming increasingly bored with school, even though he's just in third grade. I am beginning to see signs of anger and frustration. Clyde was reading second- and third-grade books by the age of four. Is it really true that gifted kids don't really need any help and they'll achieve on their own? Quite honestly, I'm beginning to worry and wonder if I should try

Figure 1.1.   Welcome to second grade, Sam.

and sell my home and move to another school district that supports gifted children!

A. I am always amazed when I hear about teachers and administrators who still actually believe gifted children will achieve to their potential without any help or guidance. In fact, I find this very frustrating and upsetting. This simply is not true. The greatest tragedy in education facing today's gifted children is the assumption that they will achieve to their full potential while being instructed at grade level!

The National Association for Gifted Children has posted eleven common myths on their website, followed with corresponding truths. I think these will help prepare you for any future meetings with Clyde's teachers. I have listed the eleven myths and truths here for you.

COMMON GIFTED EDUCATION MYTHS

Myth: Gifted students don't need help; they'll do fine on their own.

Truth: Would you send a star athlete to train for the Olympics without a coach? Gifted students need guidance from well-trained teachers who challenge and support them in order to fully develop their abilities. Many gifted students may be so far ahead of their same-age peers that they know more than half of the grade-level curriculum before the school year begins. Their resulting boredom and frustration can lead to low achievement, despondency, or unhealthy work habits. The role of the teacher is crucial for spotting and nurturing talents in school.

Myth: Teachers challenge all the students, so gifted kids will be fine in the regular classroom.

Truth: Although teachers try to challenge all students they are frequently unfamiliar with the needs of gifted children and do not know how to best serve them in the classroom. The National Research Center on Gifted and Talented (NRC/GT) found that 61 percent of teachers had no training in teaching highly able students, limiting the challenging educational opportunities offered to advanced learners. A more recent national study conducted by the Fordham Institute found that 58 percent of teachers have received no professional development focused on teaching academically advanced students in the past few years. Taken together, these reports confirm what many families have known: not all teachers are able to recognize and support gifted learners.

Myth: Gifted students make everyone else in the room smarter by providing a role model or a challenge.

Truth: In reality, average or below-average students do not look to the gifted students in the class as role models. They are more likely to model their behavior on those who have similar capabilities and are coping well in school. Seeing a student at a similar performance level succeed motivates students because it adds to their own sense of ability. Watching or relying on someone who is expected to succeed does little to increase a struggling student's sense of self-confidence. Similarly, gifted students benefit from classroom interactions with peers at similar performance levels.

Myth: All Children are gifted.

Truth: While all children are special and deserving, not all children have exceptional academic gifts that require additional or different support in school. Interestingly, most people readily accept that there are gifted children in performing arts or athletics whose talents are so far above those of others their age that they require additional or different training or coaching. It is important to understand that these same characteristics and differences apply to academically gifted students who need support and guidance to reach their full potential.

Myth: Acceleration placement options are socially harmful for gifted students.

Truth: Academically gifted students often feel bored or out of place with their age peers and naturally gravitate toward older students who are more similar as "intellectual peers." Studies have shown that many students are happier with older students who share their interest than they are with children the same age. Therefore, acceleration placement options such as early entrance to kindergarten, grade skipping, or early exit should be considered for these students.

Myth: Gifted education programs are elitist.

Truth: Gifted education is not about status; it is about meeting student needs. Advanced learners are found in all cultures, ethnic backgrounds, and socioeconomic groups. However, not every school district offers services for gifted students, even though there are gifted students in every district. Because of a lack of state and federal financial support, only affluent districts in many states can afford to offer gifted education programs and services, which leaves many gifted students behind.

Myth: That student can't be gifted; he's receiving poor grades.

Truth: Underachievement describes a discrepancy between a student's performance and his actual ability. The roots of this problem differ, based on each child's experiences. Gifted students may become bored or frustrated in an unchallenging classroom situation, causing them to lose interest, learn bad study habits, or distrust the school environment. Other students may mask their abilities to try to fit in socially with their same-age peers. No matter the cause, it is imperative that a caring and perceptive adult help gifted learners break the cycle of underachievement in order to achieve their full potential. See ERIC digests on underachievement in gifted boys and underachievement of minority students.

Myth: Gifted students are happy, popular, and well adjusted in school.

Truth: Many gifted students flourish in their community and school environment. However, some gifted children differ in terms of their emotional and moral intensity, sensitivity to expectations and feelings, perfectionism, and deep concerns about societal problems. Others do not share interests with their classmates, resulting in isolation or being labeled unfavorably as a "nerd." Because of these difficulties, the school experience is one to be endured rather than celebrated. It is estimated that 20 to 25 percent of gifted children have social and emotional difficulties, about twice as many as in the general population of students.

Myth: This child can't be gifted; he has a disability.

Truth: Some gifted students also have learning or other disabilities. These "twice-exceptional" students often go undetected in regular classrooms because their disability and gifts mask each other, making them appear "average." Other twice-exceptional students are identified as having a learning disability and, as a result, are not considered for gifted services. In both cases, it is important to focus on the students' abilities and allow them to have challenging curricula in addition to receiving help for their learning disability.

Myth: Our district has a gifted and talented program: We have AP courses.

Truth: While AP classes offer rigorous, advanced coursework, they are not a gifted education program. The AP program is designed as college-level classes taught by high school teachers for students willing to work hard. The program is limited in its service to gifted and talented students in two major areas: First,

AP is limited by the subjects offered, which in most districts is only a small handful. Second, it is limited in that typically it is offered only in high school and is generally available only for eleventh and twelfth grade students. Coupled with the one-size-fits all approach of textbooks and extensive reading lists, the limitations of AP coursework mean that districts must offer additional curriculum options to be considered as having gifted and talented services.

Myth: Gifted education requires abundant resources.

Truth: While over time, developing an effective and comprehensive gifted education program may be costly and require talented, well-qualified professionals, an abundance of resources is not necessary to begin offering gifted education services. A belief that gifted students require something different from the regular curriculum, followed by hard work and commitment from

Figure 1.2.   Why do we have to get up so early?

community and district personnel, are the most critical components in designing and implementing successful gifted education programs and services.[1]

Q. Aren't all children gifted in some way, shape, or form?

A. Absolutely! Indeed, I do believe we all have our very own special gifts. I love my gift of red hair. I love my husband's gifts of genius, exceeding generosity, and gregariousness. I love my nephew's ability to think incredibly deep. In fact, when I think of every student I've had throughout my forty-year career, I can specifically name a gift(s) he or she possesses.

I remember Sara with her most beautiful red curls and adorable freckles, Joe with his outrageous and wonderful spirit, Anne with her beautiful ballet steps, and Marie with her loving sensitivity toward me when my mother passed away. I remember equally as well Christopher, who's now a graduate from Princeton; Chip, whose own eight-year-old is exceedingly bright; and Kelly, who is pursuing a dancing career! These children and their specific gifts are but a few of the hundreds who will always remain in my heart.

We do have children in our schools whose cognitive (thinking) abilities far surpass those of their peers (classmates), and we simply must educationally serve these students! This can be done through differentiation, compacting, independent study, and acceleration combined with enrichment.

Children who are capable of high performance, whose aptitude and abilities far exceed their peers, and who are gifted need to be educated accordingly.

Q. What does the term "profoundly gifted" mean?

A. The Davidson Academy defines profoundly gifted students as individuals who score in the 99.9th percentile on IQ and achievement tests and have an exceptionally high level of intellectual prowess. These students score at least three standard deviations above the norm on the bell curve, so they are the extreme end of the intelligence, or IQ, continuum.

These students often share the following characteristics:

- An extreme need for constant mental stimulation
- An ability to learn and process complex information rapidly
- A need to explore subjects in surprising depth
- An insatiable curiosity with endless questions and inquiries
- A need for precision in thinking and expression—often answering questions with "That depends . . ."
- An ability to focus intently on a subject of interest for long periods of time
- An inability to concentrate on a task that is not intellectually challenging, including repetitious ideas or material presented in small pieces.

For more information on this topic please go to: www.ditd.org.

Q. Is stubbornness a predominant personality characteristic of highly gifted children?

A. This question brought an immense smile to my face, as I will always remember the comment my kindergarten teacher wrote to my parents on the first quarter report card going home: *Rosemary is one of the most stubborn children I have ever had as a student!* My parents' written reply was: *Yes, we know!*

Here I was at the age of six, being "sold out" to the thinking and whims of the public school system! At least, this was my interpretation then.

Nothing was written about me testing eight years beyond my peers in reading or being capable of doing math calculations equally as well! My teacher's primary concern was that I didn't/wouldn't always follow her instructions without questioning and/or offering alternatives. Of course, there are always two (or more) sides to every story, and it would be quite interesting to hear her side.

Now I'd like to think of myself as "assertive." Gifted children are often quite stubborn with a very pronounced sense of right and wrong; a sincere concern for morality, honesty, and caring; and a profound sense of justice.

I believe perfectionism tends to enhance stubbornness in gifted children as many times these children are quite intent on getting the "right answer(s)." This might also be an interfering factor in social relationships. There is more on this topic in my chapter on perfectionism.

Q. What are some of the common characteristics of gifted children?

A. Please read the list/chart I've compiled of common characteristics of gifted and talented children:

- Able to express self easily, succinctly, and without hesitation; many times we need to help them "cushion" their responses in respect for others' feelings
- Accomplished across a broad range of skills
- Can be highly opinionated
- Can be very intense
- Easy recall of facts and mastery of knowledge presented
- Enjoys detailed discussions
- Enjoys and/or even prefers adult company
- Has a broad base of knowledge—knows a large quantity of facts
- Has a delightful sense of humor and understands and appreciates wit
- Has high expectations of self and others
- Demonstrates intense concentration and attention in area(s) where interested and can become highly focused and absorbed
- Displays a keen sense of what's right and often sees issues as either black or white

- Learns quickly
- Likes to assume leadership roles
- Loves learning
- Is nonconformist
- Is observant
- Often sees things as either black or white, seldom in shades of grey
- Is a perfectionist
- Is persistent (some refer to as stubborn)
- Is questioning, curious, inquisitive
- Reads several years above grade level expectations
- Is self-critical
- Is sensitive, intuitive
- Takes pleasure in inductive learning and synthesis (creativity)
- Is verbally proficient

Q. Can you recommend any good books for me to read to help me get a better understanding of this whole arena of gifted education? What does it mean? Whom does it pertain to? Is it elitist?

A. For years, I used Gallagher and Gallagher's book, *Teaching the Gifted Child* (1994), as the main text in the graduate courses I taught. The book gave a fine overview of the academic and curricular aspects of educating the gifted. The end of each chapter contained reflective thinking questions, which I particularly liked. However, the text has become quite expensive for many struggling college students, costing more than $100 once tax is included.

I also wholeheartedly support two other textbooks in my graduate courses: Ellen Winner's *Gifted Children* (1996) and Don Treffinger's *Creative Problem Solving* (2006).

Q. I am interested in finding someone who does assessment for gifted children locally. I have eight-year-old twins; the one boy has had some assessment at school. They found that he was above 95th percentile on the Raven's Children's Colored Matrices and they suggested that I could look into the programs at Johns Hopkins. We are in a district that does not have a gifted program. I would also like to have his brother assessed, but I could not justify it with the school because he wasn't having any problems. I am also looking into local resources because I recently volunteered to be this area's gifted children's coordinator for Mensa.

A. Unfortunately, there isn't much published on identification and assessment methods for gifted children. Many schools still use IQ and achievement scores only. They are a start. Interest surveys, creativity, task commitment, achievement or the ability to achieve well beyond the norm of peers . . . all these can be fairly valid indicators of gifted abilities. For your other son, I suggest having his pediatrician write a request to the school psychologist asking to have his intelligence tested for better understanding of how to serve his intellectual and emotional needs. It may take a while, but the school will need to honor the doctor's request. Also, check the NAGC website. It is loaded with information you can use! I'll be happy to help you, so please stay in touch.

P.S. Even though your district doesn't have a "gifted program," the school district still needs to be serving all academic levels of their children, via compacting and curriculum differentiation. What works for gifted works for all.

Q. Do gifted children have the same feelings and thoughts as other children their ages?

A. All children need to be loved, protected, and nourished emotionally and intellectually. Children need to play and laugh. Children need to express themselves and have their thinking and talents supported. Gifted children

Figure 1.3.   Johnny is so smart.

are no different. Their needs are the same as those of all other children—and more.

Gifted children need to talk through the complexities in their minds. They need to listen to the adults they respect and love, heeding the wisdom and advice of caring parents and teachers. Gifted children need help with time management and organization. They need to be understood.

The Gifted Kids Survival Guide (Galbraith 1983, 17) lists the eight gripes of gifted kids, as follows:

1. The stuff we do in school is too easy and it's boring.
2. Parents (teachers and friends) expect us to be perfect, to "do our best" all the time.
3. Lots of our coursework is irrelevant.
4. Friends who *really* understand us are few and far between.
5. Peers often tease us about being smart.

Figure 1.4.   Pity the test doesn't measure all her skills.

6. We feel overwhelmed by the number of things we can do in life.
7. We feel too different, alienated.
8. We worry a lot about world problems and feel helpless to do anything.[2]

Q. Our ten-year-old daughter, Julie, was identified in kindergarten by the school district as gifted. She started reading at the age of three and excels in all subject areas. However, she does not seem to set realistic goals for herself and often doesn't complete all her projects. Is this characteristic of gifted children?

A. Yes, indeed, many gifted children want to do, see, and hear everything in sight. Because they have the ability to think and comprehend well beyond their years, these children want to experience it all, and all at once. I used to silently chuckle to myself when many of the students in my self-contained gifted classes would get teacher and parent approval for their long-term research and creativity projects, only to want to switch midstream to pursue other creative ideas!

Parents and teachers can play a huge role in helping gifted children set realistic goals, stay focused, and manage their time wisely. These skills become even more critical as children approach middle and high school years.

I deal with time management and study skills quite extensively in chapter 4. You'll find some good tips there, so keep reading.

Q. Given your expertise regarding "twice-exceptional" children, I am hoping you can point me in the right direction. My son is seventeen, a junior in high school, and highly gifted. He was tested in second grade and his IQ is 150. Typically he gets As and Bs in school depending on the quarter. Throughout his school years, my husband and I have had to prod, threaten, cajole, or do more or less whatever it takes to keep him on track. He almost never studies; he is very inconsistent when it comes to homework and assignments; he loses and misplaces things; he forgets about tests, deadlines, and due dates. Freshman year was tricky, but he seemed to buckle down and has steadily been improving and raising his grade point average. This last quarter was especially disappointing. My husband and I are both educators and understand life is more than grades; however, we see our son blessed with this brilliant brain and the potential to do so much good with it, yet he seems to be doing so little with it. He especially excels in math and chemistry. His AP chemistry teacher shared that he has never seen a student "get" what he gets, yet his test scores are mediocre (for him) at 85 percent. He feels this is too much of a discrepancy. We both believe Chris's giftedness may be camouflaging a learning disability of some sort. Chris makes careless errors on his tests—misreading directions, numbers and problems, mixing up signs, skipping problems and not noticing, missing a page or section on a test, etc. Last quarter Chris took an online class. He sat near a friend who was also taking the class. They worked together discussing ideas and content. Chris was doing great in the class. During the fifth week of instruction the teacher monitoring the class switched all the kids to different seats because she felt there was too much talking and not enough work going on. The kids were spread out and Chris had no one with whom to speak or interact. Yesterday, I received an e-mail from this teacher notifying me that Chris's grade dropped from a 95 percent to a 68 percent. His grade for the quarter is a D! When I spoke to my son and we discussed what had happened, he explained things went downhill after he was moved. He said it was hard to concentrate and stay focused. I understand to some degree, but on the other hand, I'm at a loss. If I sound a little freaked out, I am! This is such an important year for him academically. My fear is he won't be accepted into a college equipped to teach him at the level at which he is capable of being taught. As I said before, I see the gift, but of what use is it if it isn't or can't be used?

There is very little literature or material on this topic that applies specifically to my son. I'm really at a loss and hoping you may have some insights.

A. First, if Chris could start seeing a counselor who understands gifted children, that would be an immediate emotional support for him. Second, has the school tested him for dyslexia? You can request testing through the school district based on his failing grades and a registered 150 IQ. Third, perhaps his learning style is abstract random in which case study skills and organization are areas where home and school need to make modifications in helping Chris. Fourth, if you have my *Twice-Exceptional Kids* book in front of you, reread the definition of 2E on page 10. Since he's been documented as gifted (150 IQ) and obviously has some sort of learning interference, the district will need to develop a Plan 504 or IEP. This brings his teachers on board "legally" to work directly with finding and encouraging solutions to failing homework and assignments. Your local BOCES should also have someone who can test for LD if the district isn't qualified/cooperative. I believe this will be key in helping Chris. Please keep me informed as to how help for Chris progresses and please feel free to contact me with any questions or help you may need in the future.

Q. What exactly does an IQ have to do with a person being gifted? Our son measured a 128 IQ in the school testing and was denied access to the gifted program in fourth grade. Apparently, because he didn't measure an IQ of 130+, he couldn't be classified as gifted. He always earns straight As or A+s on all his tests and report cards and is considered a leader among his classmates. I'm stumped as to why Cooper would be denied entrance into the gifted program!

A. I've heard this same unfortunate story for many years throughout my career. The traditional gifted programs were set up for students who met the following three criteria:

- IQ of 130+,
- Stanines of 8 or 9 on Standardized Achievement Test scores, and
- Teacher recommendation

This was the problem with exclusive programs in the past. You were either in or out, gifted or not! While IQ (Intelligence Quotient) is a standardized measure of your potential to do well in the academic arena, it does not measure the full range of abilities, including creativity. IQ primarily measures your ability with language and numbers.

This is why an inclusive process for educating the gifted is so much better and healthier than an exclusive program in our educational system. Through the use of curriculum compacting, differentiation, and acceleration, we can service all kids, including the gifted!

Q. Our three gifted teenagers have absolutely no common sense whatsoever. I'm beginning to believe in the phrase, "If their heads weren't attached to their bodies, they'd walk off without them!" How can this be true if they're gifted?

A. If your children were right here with me now, I'd say to them, "Welcome to the club!" Giftedness has to do with the ability of children to perform or show the potential for performing at remarkably high levels of accomplishment when compared with others of their age, experience, or environment (Ross, 1993, 26).

Giftedness has nothing to do with common sense. Common sense is more than likely linked to your children's learning styles. I'm guessing their style would be abstract random.

For years when I was growing up, my father would exasperatingly say to me, "How can someone who is so smart lose so many things and not have common sense?" Being proactive, Dad put up a key ring by the door and double checked me when I arrived home to make sure I would place my keys there, otherwise I would place my keys anywhere in the house without thinking, then search frantically for them later when I needed them.

Simple but practical solutions such as this really do help children whose thinking styles are abstract random. The upside to this style is often easy ability to think "out of the box" and be creative.

Anytime you help your children with organization, time management, and just slowing them down to talk through "common sense" issues, you'll be giving them a great gift and service.

I know, I've been there, done that and was forever grateful for the help . . . still am!

Q. My husband and I are constantly at odds over our son John's seemingly inability and desire to clean up his room, desk, books, sports projects and equipment, everything really. My husband is very neat and orderly. I, on the other hand, am a lot like our son in the terms of piles and disorganization.

John is a straight A, honors student and very popular with his classmates and teachers. While he does procrastinate at times, his assignments and projects are always completed on time. My husband feels if John is a bright child, he is certainly smart enough to keep his room and life in better order and feels our son is choosing to be lazy. I've tried to explain that John is not being lazy or disrespectful. His brain and learning style are different. John and I will work together to clean up his room and within a week, everything is in disarray again. My husband wants John to get counseling, assuming something is wrong psychologically. I say no, he's a happy, smart, wonderful twelve-year-old whose mode of operation is simply opposite of my husband's. I'm simply becoming very frustrated with the standoff between my husband and son.

Any suggestions?

A. Oh my! You have the classic "standoff" between a sequential (your husband) and spatial (your son) learning style going on in your home. I can personally identify with this, as I am clearly a spatial thinker and my husband, sequential.

You can begin by Googling Linda Kreger Silverman and laughing hardily at the cartoon of a sequential learner next to a very neat and organized filing cabinet, while a spatial learner stands next to his filing cabinet, every drawer bulging with papers every which way, piles all over the top and on the floor, and papers taped to the sides. This clearly points out the primary difference between your husband and son. One way is not right and the other way wrong. It's a matter of completely different learning styles.

A learning style is everything that controls how we take in, concentrate on, understand, process, store, remember, and use new information.

Linda Kreger Silverman, Ph.D., (2002) aptly points out the plight of being nonsequential in an education world, where the school curriculum, textbooks, teachers and teaching methods, and subject mastery are sequential. Dr. Silverman directs the Institute for the Study of Advanced Development and the Gifted Development Center in Denver, Colorado. Over the past twenty-five years, Linda has focused a great deal of her work on the assessment and helping of visual-spatial learners (VSL).

May I suggest you giving Dr. Silverman's book *Upside-Down Brilliance* to your husband? The book is delightfully humorous and really does vindicate your son, you, and me, for that matter. I truly believe once your husband reads this book, he'll understand that John is not being disorderly on purpose.

Q. I was referred to you by an AGATE member. I am a parent of a highly/ profoundly gifted six-year-old and am looking for resources in the Rochester/ WNY area for parental and child support and guidance. We are also looking to find a psychologist in this area who works with gifted kids to help us with parenting issues related to behavior and so forth.

We are homeschooling our son this year after a disastrous attempt at kindergarten last year. His educational interests began at age two when he taught himself to read. He now is mainly self-taught in any topic relating to the natural sciences (dinosaurs, animals, environmental issues, prehistoric climate, atoms, cells, astronomy, etc.). At this very moment he is reading, on his own, an article in *Scientific American* on optical illusions. We have had many problems socializing him to age peers due to behavior/tantrums and lack of interest on his part.

If you have any information or suggestions for these questions, I'd be so very happy to hear them. It has been incredibly difficult to find a community for us.

Figure 1.5.   What are you doing?

A. Let me begin by complimenting you on having a profoundly gifted child! That being said, I hope I can lend you some help in bringing more happiness and social/academic adjustments for him. A website that could be useful to you is at the Davidson Academy for the Profoundly Gifted in Nevada at www.DavidsonGifted.org. As you peruse this website, you'll glean comfort in knowing you're not alone and that there is understanding and help for wonderfully bright children like your son!

I hope this is a bit of help for you. Please feel free to contact me with any questions or thoughts you think I might be able to help you with.

In closing this chapter, I would like to reference Rita and Ken Dunn's work on learning styles. The Dunn's combined publications include twelve books and more than two hundred and fifty book chapters, articles, research papers, and monographs (Dunn and Dunn, 1993). The Dunn and Dunn Learning Styles Model has gained popular acceptance and use in K–12, its primary goal to improve effectiveness of instruction through the identification and matching of individual learning styles with appropriate learning opportunities.

NOTES

1. Archambault, F. S., Westberg, K. L., Brown, S. W., Hallmark, B. W., Emmons, C. L., and Zhang, W. (1993). *Regular Classroom Practices with Gifted Students: Results of a National Survey of Classroom Teachers* (#93102). Storrs, CT: The National Research Center on the Gifted and Talented.

2. Excerpted from *The Gifted Kids' Survival Guide for Ages 11-18,* by Judy Galbraith, © 1983. Free Publishing, Inc., Minneapolis, MN, 800-735-7323.

Chapter Two

Programming and Curriculum Development in Gifted Education

Too often children are given answers to remember rather than problems to solve.

—Robert Lewin

There are a variety of program models and curriculum developments that have developed over the past two decades to help in the appropriate education of our high achieving, cognitively gifted students. Ideally, your school district is providing training and assistance to your teachers so that all students may benefit from these advances.

Following is a list of several program models and curriculum development for educating the gifted for your knowledge base.

ACCELERATION

This refers to moving the student to a level of study that matches his or her aptitude and mastery levels in one or more curricular areas. Acceleration may be content-based, including strategies of:

- Curriculum compacting
- Single-subject acceleration
- Dual enrollment
- Credit by examination or prior experience
- Advanced placement
- International Baccalaureate programs
- Talent search programs

Grade-based acceleration strategies may include:

* Early entrance to school
* Whole grade acceleration
* Grade telescoping
* Early entrance to college

I personally love curriculum compacting. It can be highly effective and makes so much sense.

ADVANCED PLACEMENT COURSES

AP courses were originally designed to provide gifted students with the opportunity to receive college-level-course credit while still in high school. Educational Testing Service provides an opportunity for students to take a test in a specified subject area and students will usually receive college credit if they score either a 4 or 5.

BEST PRACTICES IN GIFTED EDUCATION

Best practices refer to techniques and methods that seem to be more effective at helping to deliver a desired outcome.

One of the assignments for my graduate students is requiring everyone to review the chart of best practices in Ann Robinson's 2006 text, *Best Practices in Gifted Education*. Research based, the twenty-nine practices included have been tested and shown to work with gifted students.

Subsequently, I ask the students to develop their own best practices chart, based on their professional experiences in the classroom and what they've learned in my courses.

Following is a chart summarizing the best of my students' best practices. I hope you'll be able to draw from these as a parent and/or educator.

BLOOM'S TAXONOMY

Benjamin Bloom had such a wonderful impact on the enhancement of thinking and use of higher-order thinking skills since he first published his taxonomy of the Cognitive Domain. I still tell my students that taking all of their students to the synthesis and evaluation levels of thinking is absolutely key in educating the gifted and all children!

Table 2.1. Best Practices

Home	Classroom	School
• Environment of acceptance and tolerance	• Curriculum compacting	• Advanced placement classes/honors courses/college credit
• Encourage social consciousness	• Curriculum mapping	• Professional development courses
• Read to your children and vice versa	• Encourage creativity	• Career education
• Designate a reading time	• Classroom collaboration—teacher/student/parents/administration	• Diversity education
• Provide opportunities to explore community and travel	• Differentiation	• Peer mentoring
• Encourage meaningful socialization with a diverse range of adults and children	• Classroom blogging and web research	• Support a gifted student support team
• Help with time management skills	• SQ3R	• Independent study program
• Provide atmosphere for creativity	• Teach and promote	• Encourage extracurricular activities
• Discussion and guidance with social-emotional issues and peer relationships	• Higher-level thinking skills	• Provide internships
• Family discussions of current events	• Multiple intelligences	• Liaisons with local colleges and universities
• Encourage volunteering, helping others, service	• Inquiry-based learning and teaching	• Elimination of classes with excess review and drill problems when it is not needed
• Promote balance of activities—downtime, fun, household responsibilities, school work, exercise, family discussions	• Incorporate as many forms of technology into the lessons whenever possible and applicable	• Provide opportunities after school for tutoring and additional learning
• Seek mentors and role models	• Study skills	• Offer a variety of electives
• Secondary language development	• Independent study	• National and international competitions
	• Teach writing "from the heart, first, mind second"	• Integration of the arts across the curriculum
	• Instruction that has utility and purpose from the students' perspective	• Variety of extracurricular activities
	• Varied assessment strategies—formative and summative	• Interdisciplinary curriculum/provide time for planning and team teaching
	• Student-centered learning	• Community service programs
		• Challenging curriculum
		• Programs to teach problem-solving skills
		• Internship opportunities with the university

Chapter Two

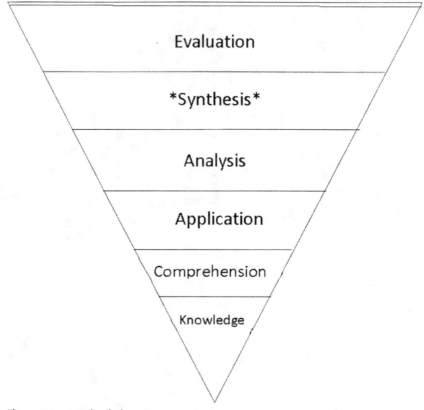

Figure 2.1. Levels of Bloom's Taxonomy

The first three levels of thinking suggest an easy repetitive level of thought processing in supporting memorization, recall, discussion, and problem solving.

The second three higher levels of thinking promote a more personal, complex, interrelated reflection of learning, where synthesis makes learning personal and more realistic for the student.

In 2001, a group of educators revised the basic taxonomy, interchanging remember for knowledge, understanding for comprehension, and apply for application, while topping the order with create after evaluation (Anderson et al., 2001).

In both models I have starred the synthesis/create higher level of thinking. In my experience, synthesis is the key and joy to learning for all of our students.

I clearly remember working with a team of middle school educators where the principal decided to require the team to develop an integrated unit for the

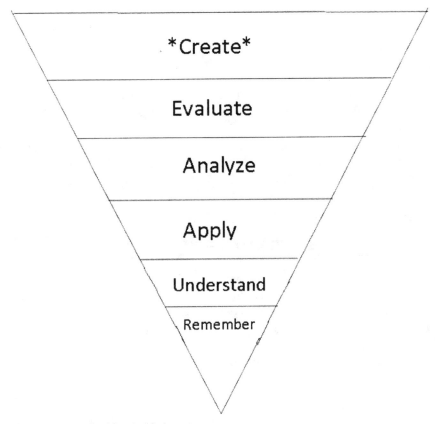

Figure 2.2. Revised levels of Bloom's taxonomy.

obvious benefit of the seventh-grade students, rather than teaching independently of each other.

As you can well imagine, teacher resistance on a scale of 1 to 10, 10 being the highest, was about a 25. Each teacher was very protective of his or her own domain. Initially, I think a dentist would have had an easier time pulling teeth than I had encouraging the teachers to work together!

After several team meetings, the overall integrative project began to gel. Rather than teaching specific dates, battles, towns, generals of the Civil War, the grade-level team began to look at reflections of civil wars worldwide. Newbery books such as *My Brother Sam Is Dead* took on a new meaning. Music themes linked tragedy, harmony, morals, and human resiliency into human strength and community awareness.

Once separate English and social studies classes became linked and team taught, students started expressing real pleasure in going to classes. Vocabulary words from the units were heard in classes throughout the day.

With the expectation that all levels of students in the seventh grade would demonstrate their personal strengths and learning at the synthesis level, a weeklong culmination of student projects went on display and were actively presented. Songs were composed, poetry written, uniforms designed, bibliographies developed, dances demonstrated, plays written and acted—on and on the list of activities went. I can honestly say the middle school was abuzz from the excitement with an integrated grade-level study of Reflections on Civil Wars!

I encourage parents as well as teachers to become familiar with Bloom's Taxonomy in the hopes that we can all encourage our children in the vocabulary, thinking, and expectations of higher-level thinking skills. Application, evaluation, and synthesis truly do make learning joyful and rewarding!

CHARTER SCHOOLS

Charter schools provide parents with alternative choices for their children's education and operate with freedom from many of the requirements and regulations of traditional public schools. The three main reasons for founding charter schools are to realize an educational vision, gain autonomy, and serve a special population. An important benefit of charter schools is the increased opportunity and freedom for learning, specific to the needs and choices of its students. As I support homeschooling as an important and other wonderful alternative education, I also wholeheartedly support the concept of charter schools.

CONSULTANT TEACHER

This model provides the classroom teacher and gifted students with an education expert right in the classroom, servicing a direct support for instruction.

CURRICULUM COMPACTING

Students may pretest out of units of study they already have mastered at an earlier time in their educational development than their peers. This gives the children time to pursue other studies of interest or more advanced materials in the curriculum being currently studied. Curriculum compacting also gives time and freedom to students whose achievement(s) is above grade-level expectations.

CURRICULUM DIFFERENTIATION

Curriculum differentiation is a teaching approach that focuses on the higher-level thinking skills of application, synthesis, and evaluation and can be applied in the educational areas of content, process, and product in the learning environment. Teachers respond to where students' mastery levels are, not at grade-level expectations.

Every semester, I excitedly tell my graduate students that we'll start to focus on curriculum differentiation the second week of class and this will be the major and most exciting key for working with gifted children and all children.

I've seen curriculum differentiation become more and more complex over the years with a myriad of textbooks and courses being offered to unravel the many strategies associated with differentiation. I believe it doesn't have to be as complicated as it now can seem.

Quite simply, curriculum differentiation is an art form. Coupled with the synthesis level of Bloom's Taxonomy, we can provide the keys to personal, creative, and joyful learning to all students. If want you to go more in-depth on the topic, there are many books and courses devoted solely to this topic.

Tomlinson (1999) gives a nice summary of the elements of differentiation principles that guide responses to students' learning differences.

- The Teacher Focuses on the Essentials. Clarity increases the likelihood that a teacher can introduce a subject in a way that each student finds meaningful and interesting.
- The Teacher Attends to Student Differences. Children search for the sense of triumph that comes when they are respected, valued, nurtured, and even cajoled into accomplishing things they believed beyond their grasp.
- Assessment and Instruction Are Inseparable. Formative Assessment always has more to do with helping students grow than with cataloging their mistakes.
- The Teaching Modifies Content Process and Products. Teachers may adapt one or more of the curricular elements (content, process, products) based on one or more of the student characteristics (readiness, interest, learning profile) at any point in a lesson or unit.
- All Students Participate in Respectful Work. There is a deep respect for the identity of the individual.
- The Teacher and Student Collaborate in Learning. A differentiated classroom is of necessity student-centered. Students are the workers. The teacher coordinates time, space, materials, and activities.
- The Teacher Balances Group and Individual Norms. A great coach never achieves greatness for himself or his team by working to make all his players

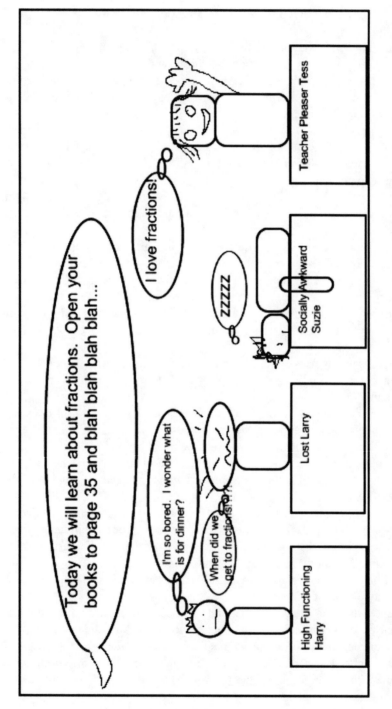

Figure 2.3. A classroom without differential instruction is a classroom with differentiated attention, motivation, and learning! Drawn by R. Gammiero

alike. To be great, he must make each player the best that he or she possibly can be.

• The Teacher and Students Work Together Flexibly. The goal is to link learners with essential understandings and skills at appropriate levels of challenge and interest.

ENRICHMENT IN REGULAR CLASSROOM

Enrichment refers to the classroom teacher providing additional work and/or activities/materials for individual students who already have mastered the grade-level materials. I caution teachers not to always assign additional work at learning centers in the room once a child has completed his work. Otherwise being bright seems to incur a punishment of having to do more work. Allowing student choice can be huge in supporting the joy of learning in students.

INDEPENDENT STUDY

Guided and directed by the teacher, an independent study can provide a wonderful opportunity for a student to develop an interest or talent that may not be provided in the regular curriculum. This *does not* mean sending gifted students off on their own unsupervised, without instruction, guidance, and help.

INTERNATIONAL BACCALAUREATE

The International Baccalaureate (IB) is an international foundation headquartered in Geneva, Switzerland. IB offers three educational programs for children ages three to nineteen: Primary Years (PYP), Middle Years (MYP), and Diploma Programme (DD). The International Baccalaureate aims to develop inquiring, knowledgeable, and caring young people who help to create a better and more peaceful world through intercultural understanding and respect.

MENTORS

A mentor is a wonderful "gift" for any child. A student(s) may access a mentor by leaving the school on a specific day or days for a specified amount of time. The mentor is a specialist in the area of expertise or focused interest of

the child. I dearly wish I had a mentor growing up. What a gift that would
have been!

MODEL UNITED NATIONS

Model United Nations (MUN) is an academic simulation of the United Nations whose focus is to educate student participants about civics, current
events, effective communication, globalization, and multilateral diplomacy.
Students research countries, act as diplomats, and develop solutions to world
problems in the simulations. While I never participated in the Model Union,
I would want every single one of my students to embrace this opportunity.
What a wonderful way to broaden one's perspective, understanding diplomacy and enhancement of the world. Go, Model UN!

RESOURCE ROOM

This model reminds me of the classic quote, "Help! I'm gifted more than one
hour a week!" This is the criticism most often levied against the resource
room model, where gifted students are pulled out of their regular classrooms
a specified amount of time per day or week. A teaching expert provides direct
instruction for the gifted students. Many times students are required to make
up the work they missed in the regular classroom while they were gone. Thus,
the resource room model can become a punishment for being gifted.

RESPONSE TO INTERVENTION (RTI)

When Congress reauthorized the Individuals with Disabilities Act (IDEA),
educators were required to identify all struggling learners (not just special
education students) and be responsible to their needs before their failure.

As a model for remediation, RTI is based on a pyramid of interventions,
giving appropriate support to students based on their achievement levels in
the core academic areas of reading, writing, and math.

RTI also provides a compelling framework for improving behavior, at-
tendance, and school completion. This may also require the enrichment of
students in order to ensure their success as well.

Eventually I am sure we'll have gathered reams of evidence and successful
anecdotes of RTI supporting the success of our twice-exceptional students
throughout our school populations.

SPECIAL SCHOOLS

Special schools provide a secondary education for high-ability, high-achieving students.

Q. The school district my three children are in is constantly fighting over how to best service gifted children. Many of the parents want their children identified, pulled out, and serviced in a self-contained classroom. Teachers want the students to remain in their own classrooms. What is the best way to educate gifted children? I don't want my children losing out.

A. Good news. It doesn't matter how your gifted children are serviced for their best education. It *does matter* that they *are*! A three-year study in Framingham, Massachusetts, looked at educating gifted children, using three program models. In 1984, the National Diffusion Network published the results from this study that compared the effectiveness of these three major program models used in delivering Project SAGE instruction to academically gifted students: separate classrooms (self-contained), resource room, and the consultant teacher model (Cymerman and Modest, 1984).

The research found that students who participated in the pilot program, using all three program models, performed at a significantly higher level

WHO MURDERED THE MINDS OF GIFTED CHILDREN?

PROFESSOR DULL, IN THE CLASSROOM, WITH REPETITIVE DRILLS

Figure 2.4.   Who murdered the minds of gifted children?

in higher-order thinking skills and academics than their peers in the control group who did not receive special services.

So, you see, schools can use a variety of program models to provide appropriate instruction for gifted students. The key is *providing* the *instruction*!

Q. All four of our children went through a self-contained gifted program in a suburban district of Rochester, New York. While my husband and I were very happy with the teachers and education our children received, the students certainly were very isolated from the remainder of the school population and it was obvious there was open disdain (jealousy) toward the gifted class from the other students and teachers. How do you feel about self-contained gifted classes and their effect on the social interaction and development of self and peer relationships?

A. Your situation is of particular interest to me since I started my teaching career with gifted education in a fourth-grade self-contained classroom. The students selected for the program were bused from all over the district to my classroom.

As an educator, I believed this program model was an excellent way to service the academic and emotional needs of gifted children, and in many ways, it was. However, the resentment of other teachers toward a classroom of gifted students was enormous. The disdain was not just covert; it was blatantly overt! The unfriendliness from parents of children who were not selected for this district's gifted program was just as bad or worse!

Few teachers who chose to teach in the district's gifted program lasted more than one, two, or three years because of the prejudice and isolation.

I survived eighteen years. I believed that all children deserved to become all they are capable of becoming, including very bright children, and I was willing to suffer the indignities of others to support my beliefs and the educational rights of these children.

The self-contained gifted program became such a "hot bed" of political uproar that the district finally did away with it in the 1990s.

I continued to educationally serve the gifted students and all the students in my heterogeneously grouped classrooms both at the elementary and middle school levels.

I clearly remember the resource room teacher saying to me, "Now that you'll be having a heterogeneously grouped classroom, you'll find that you'll be spending an inordinate amount of time with the slower-achieving students."

My mental response was, "Over my dead body!" You see, I believed in giving equal amounts of time to my students. I would certainly "help" the slower-achieving students, but I would also "help" the higher-achieving students whom I was trying to educate at the appropriate instructional levels. To do less was unacceptable in my mind.

As time progressed, I came to support an inclusive process for the education of gifted students, rather than an exclusive program. This process was a healthier approach community-wide. Rather than being *in* or *out*, *gifted* or *not gifted*, the inclusive process did not *exclude* children and families; rather, it *included* and *encompassed* the districtwide community.

A large number of my former "self-contained" gifted students and their parents have kept in touch with me. We're all pretty much in agreement that while a self-contained program academically serves gifted children, emotionally it seems to encourage negative issues with staff, other students, and administrators—for the teacher of self-contained gifted as well as the students.

Serving the Gifted:
An
Inclusive Process
Rather than
An

Exclusive Program!

Q. Can you explain to me what curriculum compacting is?

A. Sure. So many of our gifted children daily suffer the indignities of doing curricular work and endless hours of homework on material they already know. In fact, research on curriculum compacting shows that teachers could eliminate as much as 40 to 50 percent of the usual material without affecting achievement scores in reading, math, computation, social studies, and spelling (Reis, 1994). Basically, curriculum compacting excuses high-ability students from plowing through material they have already mastered.

Curriculum compacting is one of the major components in serving the instruction and education needs of gifted children, eliminating repetitive work that students have previously mastered. It provides an easy and accountable process for students who already know most of their grade-level content.

Not surprising to many educators or parents of gifted children, the National Commission on Excellence in Education released a searing report in 1983 on the condition of American educational institutions, finding that 50 percent of all gifted students did not perform to their tested potential.

Curriculum compacting is a wonderful strategy used by gifted education specialists to service not only high-achieving students, but all students whose abilities and/or achievements surpass those of their grade-level peers. By using compacting, students' achievements are assessed by pretesting their curriculum knowledge before a unit of study. Why make children study materials they already know and have mastered? To me, this is pure common sense! The educator can then set up a plan of study to include materials the student may not already know and develop units of study to challenge and develop the child's cognitive base. This is where a blend of enrichment and acceleration complement educational excellence for our country's children.

Tannenbaum has advocated a similar process called telescoping in which students "complete the basics in the least amount of time, thereby sparing themselves the tedium of dwelling on content that they either know already or can absorb in short order" (1986, 409).

Reis, Burns, and Renzulli (1992, 5–8) refer to curriculum compacting as a process in which a teacher preassesses students' skills or knowledge about content prior to instruction and uses this information to modify curriculum. Their eight-part process of compacting includes the following:

1. Identify the relevant learning objectives in a subject area or grade level.
2. Find appropriate pretests.
3. Identify students who should be pretested.
4. Pretest students to determine mastery levels of the chosen objectives.
5. Eliminate instructional time for students who show mastery of these objectives.
6. Streamline instruction of those objectives students have not yet mastered but are capable of mastering more quickly than their classmates.
7. Offer challenging alternatives for time provided by compacting.
8. Keep records of this process and the instructional options available to the selected students.

I love curriculum compacting! It makes so much sense, especially in this day and age of inclusion classrooms, where teachers are spread very thin and gifted students are still often used as tutors for the slower-achieving students. I encourage all my graduate students to learn, use, and maintain compacting as an excellent strategy in their classrooms and support of their school district's dedication to educate all their children, including their gifted.

As the district coordinator for gifted K–8, I would meet with the teachers regularly at each grade level and together we would determine who might need curriculum compacting. Many times I would do the pretesting, then compile the activities and study packets for the students at the appropriate instructional levels. This saved the classroom teachers a great deal of time and often I would do mini-lessons to support the information contained in the packets.

Even if an enrichment specialist is not available to help teachers with curriculum compacting, it is clearly an excellent and viable part of the overall education of gifted children and well worth the initial time and effort it takes to initiate.

Q. Does differentiation serve the needs of the gifted? Our district's entire focus in their gifted program is differentiation. Is that all there is?

A. Differentiation is a *part* of the process needed to service the educational needs of gifted children, not the complete process. Just as districts in the '70s, '80s, and '90s went overboard with enrichment as the answer for educating gifted children, school districts are now going overboard with differentiation as the sole answer for educating gifted children. Another key part of the process is servicing gifted children at their aptitude levels, which could entail acceleration, compacting, enrichment, and/or possible grade skipping.

When you have a second grader whose reading comprehension and vocabulary levels are at the eighth-grade level, exposing him/her to more and more books at the second-grade reading level is *not* going to expand the student's cognitive learnings, nor is it going to expand his or her vocabulary and comprehension.

Until we can help teachers and administrators feel more comfortable with compacting and acceleration at the elementary and middle school levels, I do not believe we are fully servicing our gifted children. At the high school level, AP (Advanced Placement) courses are readily acceptable.

Differentiation is a start. Credit goes to *your* school district for supporting it. Encourage them to expand their process for servicing their gifted.

Q. How do you know if you are challenging your gifted students?

A. This is a genuine and common concern of many teachers who are currently being overburdened with inclusion classrooms whose numbers exceed twenty-five-plus children with academic and aptitude ranges varying from three to five years below grade level up to eight to ten years beyond grade level. Ideally, districts are providing aides and gifted and talented facilitators to help these teachers with curriculum compacting and differentiation as a start.

You know you are not challenging your gifted students if you are:

1. Having them help the slower-achieving students in the classroom on a regular or daily basis,
2. Having them do grade-level work and they almost always finish first or before most of their classmates,
3. If you give them "enrichment" activities that are always at grade-level expectations,
4. If they are getting straight As in achievement because they already know the material being taught,

5. If their writing and speaking reflect "rote memorization," and . . .
6. If the work they are producing is at the lower level of thinking on Bloom's Taxonomy—knowledge, comprehension, and application.

You are challenging your gifted students if you are:

1. Pretesting their knowledge base and compacting their curriculum so they are learning at their aptitude and achievement levels,
2. If you are considering the alternatives of enrichment combined with acceleration and grade-level curriculum,
3. If they are spending somewhat equal amounts of time in class learning and completing appropriate assignments as their peers achieving at grade level,
4. If their writing and speaking reflect a higher-level thinking order, and . . .
5. If the work they are producing is at the higher level of Bloom's Taxonomy—analysis, synthesis, and evaluation.

I've known some districts that differentiate their curriculum for the benefit of their gifted students and expect only these children to produce at the application, synthesis, and evaluation levels, while the other students are not expected to achieve at these levels at all! Here we should revise our thinking, as I truly believe we should be training and expecting *all* of our students to produce at these higher levels of thinking!

Q. My son always finishes his work ahead of the rest of his class, so the teacher uses him as a helper/tutor for the other children. While I encourage Colton to be kind and helpful, shouldn't he be working on his own projects and interests while he's waiting for his classmates to finish their assignments?

A. Yes! Helping others is certainly a valuable, caring, and necessary activity for all of us throughout our lives. In school, such behavior should be encouraged and respected. However, if done to the exclusion of self-achievement and learning and being taught at the appropriate ability level, it is not right. If we rob Peter to pay Paul, where is the justice for Peter? If Colton is "tutoring/helping" his classmates daily, where is his educational justice in the development of his abilities?

Compacting and small group instruction should begin for Colton and other high-achieving children as early as kindergarten. It's their educational right.

Q. My child comes home every day from kindergarten and asks me why she can't learn something new in school. She used to be a very happy and bubbly little girl. Now she's losing her enthusiasm for school. Eugenia was

Figure 2.5. Today's current lesson.

reading by the time she was three years old. In school she must sit through daily lessons on the letters of the alphabet. When I've talked to her teacher about this, she says kindergarten is a time to learn socialization skills and there are far too many students for her (the teacher) to do individual lessons with my child. Can't something be done to help with the education of the five-year-olds that already get along with their peers and know the curriculum two or three years before entering school? This just doesn't seem fair nor right. Do you agree?

A. I not only agree with you, I truly empathize with you and feel your frustration as a parent and a teacher. I am saddened by the number of schools that do not provide an education for students at their appropriate aptitude and achievement levels. We've come way too far with Bloom's Taxonomy, differentiation models, gifted program models, compacting, acceleration, independent study, learning centers, and so on to have children repeating skills and academics in school they've learned months or years before.

While I do empathize with the increasing load and expectations placed on teachers in our classrooms from year to year, there are staff development courses available and consultants who can readily be hired to come into districts and actually help the educators with initial compacting and differentiation.

Many districts are now hiring gifted and talented coordinators to help with district curriculum development, teaching training, and student support. Beware of a district coordinator who doesn't want to work with the children at all. This may indicate a "hands off" rather than "hands on" philosophy.

> I believe all kids deserve the right to the best education, an education that
> suits them, and gifted kids are no exception.
>
> —Stephen Pulford, Ph.D.

Q. It seems that our school district focuses on "enrichment" activities to fulfill its obligations to our gifted children. In mathematics, my son has scored eight years beyond his grade-level peers. Doesn't it make sense he should be doing math work at a more difficult and more complex level other than enrichment exercises at his fourth-grade level?

A. Absolutely! In a positive sense, enrichment activities are meant to extend the curriculum and regular school day programs, providing more in-depth experiences, uses of creativity, *and* thought-provoking exercises. In theory, enrichment would benefit any child. In practice, many school districts have gone overboard with the use of "enrichment" as the sole means of servicing its gifted population. I have seen many gifted elementary students over the years "enriched" with grade-level activities until the children wanted to regurgitate. Finishing their work ahead of their peers became a "punishment" for gifted kids. They would be expected to move onto one of the "enrichment centers" and do "more work" or be expected to help the slower-achieving students, thus diminishing the positive effects of completing the required assignment or project.

This use of enrichment is often controlled by the teacher and seldom gives the high-achieving student time to pursue his or her own interests and talents.

We need to look at a balance. There are hundreds of thousands of exceptional learning or enrichment centers throughout the classrooms in our country's schools. They should be a "part of" the students' day or a viable option, not a must once the day's activities are completed.

If we are educating our gifted students at their appropriate aptitude levels, via compacting or acceleration, for example, then it would be highly unlikely that these children would be finishing their daily assignments so far ahead of their peers. And if they do, why not let them choose how they would like to spend the additional time while their peers are completing their assignments? If someone loves to read, let him or her read. If Mark loves writing computer programs, why not let him work on the computer? If Olivia is a gifted artist, let her work on her illustration on the easel in the art room the art teacher has provided for her. And if John is simply tired, putting his head down for fifteen minutes on his desk and napping could refresh him physically and mentally for the remainder of the day!

Figure 2.6. Jenny, can you come and help us?

Q. While I credit our school district with trying to service gifted children, the process seems to be failing at the elementary and middle school levels. Even the AP courses at the high school seem to pile on more and more work, without giving equivalent grade point averages. Our daughter is a very gifted writer and is becoming frustrated with the additional writing assignments she is given because of her talent. At this point, I'm willing to homeschool, but I'm afraid Meghan will miss out on social and peer relationships. Please advise.

A. I certainly can support your decision to homeschool after having a very brilliant graduate student in one of my graduate classes who was homeschooling her own two very gifted children. Until that time, I must confess, I was a product of many of the same stereotypes that educators and the general public have about homeschooling.

Every semester, I always invited three homeschooling parents in for a presentation to my graduate students in "Teaching the Gifted K–12." My students always raved about the session for weeks that followed.

Suzanne ran a very structured learning day for her elementary-aged children, with subject instruction scheduled at certain times and a mini-classroom set up in her basement.

Shelly's children's days were unstructured. Her middle and high school children (as well as she) sleep into a natural waking each morning. The children and their mother have a quiet part of the house to study, create, read, and so on. Mutually agreed-upon times are issued when help with instruction will be given. Trips to the local library or museums can be all day, to benefit each family member.

Jennifer homeschooled for religious and family reasons. Her two high school children were attending the public school and were academic and social leaders in their classes. Jennifer's sixth grader is being homeschooled and "aces" the state and district tests she takes at home each year.

Academic and social events are scheduled regularly for homeschoolers throughout the county. The myth that homeschoolers would miss the socialization acquired in public schools just isn't true. I was awed by the number of events and volunteer time donated for the benefit of all homeschooled children by these parents.

I respect homeschooling as a positive and family-oriented alternative for the education of your children. I encourage you to try it if that's where your heart is leaning.

Q. The staff development monies in our district are being used almost exclusively for the training of teachers in 4 MAT. Everyone is expected to speak and write using the 4 MAT lingo, to the exclusion of all else. Is this training model the best way to educate gifted children?

A. No. 4 MAT is one of many excellent program models being used to en-hance educators' understanding and development of children's and adults' learning styles as well as teaching strategies. I would be a bit leery of any district that promotes one style of teacher training to the exclusion of all others. It's a little bit like expecting all children to think and produce the same way, the opposite of what education should be doing—enhancing the thinking, production, and creativity of the individual at his or her best levels.

I encourage you to encourage your children's school district to be more flexible in its teaching training regimen. There are many excellent methods and techniques available to use in the educating of our children. Some meth-ods work for some; others work equally as well or better for others. Good luck!

Q. My child has been tested to be reading at the sixth-grade comprehension level, yet she is forced to read the same curricular materials as the other stu-dent peers in the second-grade classroom. How can I get instructional help for her to ensure she's extending her knowledge and ability base?

A. Don't despair. There are a variety of supplemental reading programs that I have used very successfully throughout my career to enhance gifted and independent readers. One of them is Accelerated Reader. Accelerated Reader is a sensory information system that manages literature-based reading practice. With more than 30,000 titles for children to select from, this easily accessible software program supports the actual reading level of participating students. Children in first grade whose cognitive reading level far surpasses their peers by two, three, four, or even five years needn't by slowed down by "grade-level" reading lessons and expectations. The same is true for all the other elementary, middle, and high school level children.

While Accelerated Reader was first designed as a software literature pro-gram for gifted children, it has now expanded to support test scores for all levels.

Q. Do you have any favorite books you could recommend for my eleven-year-old son to read? He is always so busy completing daily homework as-signments, he doesn't have time for pleasure reading. The little time he does have, the books need to be good! He used to love pleasure reading. Help!

A. YES! I absolutely love and adore the Newbery books and I think parents would enjoy reading these yearly award-winning books right along with their children. The reading levels range approximately between 4.5 and 6.0 and I've used some of the titles with gifted second- and third-grade readers as well as middle school children.

NEWBERY AWARD–WINNING BOOKS

The Newbery Award for original and creative work in the field of children's books was first awarded in 1922 to Hendrik Willem van Loon for *The Story of Mankind*. Since its inception, seventy-nine award-winning books and well over two hundred honor books have received the prestigious John Newbery Medal.

My personal all-time Newbery favorite is Robert C. O'Brien's *Mrs. Frisby and the Rats of NIMH*, followed by Spinelli's *Maniac Magee,* Paterson's *Bridge to Terabithia*, and Raskin's, *The Westing Game*. I've read all the Newberys.

I still remember sitting up in bed exclaiming, "No, please, no!" when Leslie accidentally died in *Terabithia*. Every year I read *Mrs. Frisby* to my classes, whether teaching middle school level, intermediate, or primary children and the students loved it.

The Newbery books present dilemmas, problem solving, life experiences, family support, and interactions with enriched vocabulary, ad infinitum. I've yet to meet a gifted student who wasn't intrigued and delighted with the Newbery books.

While I was teaching a self-contained fourth-grade class of gifted students (many years ago), I developed a Newbery Club to accelerate reading of fine literature in my classroom. I applied to our school's PTA for a $300 grant to get started and received it. With parent volunteers, we began by modeling a Newbery membership card after our school's computer club membership card. We made twenty-five buttons with our school's button machine, using a picture of the Newbery bronze medal designed by René Paul Chambellan back in 1921.

Great news! Within two years, the Newbery Club became a schoolwide incentive reading program for our fourth, fifth, and sixth grades, sponsored by the profits from the library's yearly book fair. We also had third graders reading Newberys, as well as five gifted second graders. In fact, one of the third graders broke all the school records initially established and received all the prizes we had to offer by the end of fourth grade. We reworked the award system and extended the top award to the reading of 150 Newbery books and prizes that could be accumulative throughout the child's schooling! The Newbery Club became a wonderful, schoolwide, outstanding reading incentive!

I have included a copy of our original Newbery Club Award Sheet and an overview of the John Newbery Award. I've also provided a listing of the award winning books, 1922–2009, for you.

Happy reading-and-awarding!

* * * AWARDS * * *

Newbery Club Book Awards

READ! READ! READ!

READ/CONFERENCE		PRIZES	
I.	3 Books	I.	A Membership Card and Newbery Button
II.	6 Books	II.	1 Free Newbery Book of Your Choice
III.	10 Books	III.	1 More Fabulous, Exciting, Adventurous Newbery Book!!!
IV.	15 Books	IV.	1 Cool Newbery T-Shirt!
V.	25 Books	V.	2 More Newbery Books!
VI.	35 Books	VI.	Another 2 Books!!
VII.	50 Books	VII.	3 Free Books and an Ice Cream Sundae of your Choice
VIII.	65 Books	VIII.	2 Free Newberys
XI.	80 Books	XI.	A Trophy
X.	90 Books	X.	3 Free Books
XI.	100 Books	XI.	1 Free Book for the Remainder of the School Year!

CONGRATULATIONS !

Figure 2.7. Newbery Book Club awards.

Newbery Medal Winners, 1922–2009:

- 2009: *The Graveyard Book* by Neil Gaiman, illus. by Dave McKean (HarperCollins)
- 2008: *Good Masters! Sweet Ladies! Voices from a Medieval Village* by Laura Amy Schlitz (Candlewick)
- 2007: *The Higher Power of Lucky* by Susan Patron, illus. by Matt Phelan (Simon & Schuster/Richard Jackson)
- 2006: *Criss Cross* by Lynne Rae Perkins (Greenwillow Books/HarperCollins)
- 2005: *Kira-Kira* by Cynthia Kadohata (Atheneum Books for Young Readers/Simon & Schuster)
- 2004: *The Tale of Despereaux: Being the Story of a Mouse, a Princess, Some Soup, and a Spool of Thread* by Kate DiCamillo (Candlewick Press)
- 2003: *Crispin: The Cross of Lead* by Avi (Hyperion Books for Children)
- 2002: *Single Shard* by Linda Park (Houghton Mifflin)
- 2001: *Year Down Yonder* by Richard Peck (Dial Publishers)
- 2000: *Bud, Not Buddy* by Christopher Paul Curtis (Delacorte)
- 1999: *Holes* by Louis Sachar (Frances Foster)
- 1998: *Out of the Dust* by Karen Hesse (Scholastic)
- 1997: *The View from Saturday* by E. L. Konigsburg (Jean Karl/Atheneum)
- 1996: *The Midwife's Apprentice* by Karen Cushman (Clarion)
- 1995: *Walk Two Moons* by Sharon Creech (HarperCollins)
- 1994: *The Giver* by Lois Lowry (Houghton)
- 1993: *Missing May* by Cynthia Rylant (Jackson/Orchard)
- 1992: *Shiloh* by Phyllis Reynolds Naylor (Atheneum)
- 1991: *Maniac Magee* by Jerry Spinelli (Little, Brown)
- 1990: *Number the Stars* by Lois Lowry (Houghton)
- 1989: *Joyful Noise: Poems for Two Voices* by Paul Fleischman (Harper)
- 1988: *Lincoln: A Photobiography* by Russell Freedman (Clarion)
- 1987: *The Whipping Boy* by Sid Fleischman (Greenwillow)
- 1986: *Sarah, Plain and Tall* by Patricia MacLachlan (Harper)
- 1985: *The Hero and the Crown* by Robin McKinley (Greenwillow)
- 1984: *Dear Mr. Henshaw* by Beverly Cleary (Morrow)
- 1983: *Dicey's Song* by Cynthia Voigt (Atheneum)
- 1982: *A Visit to William Blake's Inn: Poems for Innocent and Experienced Travelers* by Nancy Willard (Harcourt)
- 1981: *Jacob Have I Loved* by Katherine Paterson (Crowell)
- 1980: *A Gathering of Days: A New England Girl's Journal, 1830–1832* by Joan W. Blos (Scribner)
- 1979: *The Westing Game* by Ellen Raskin (Dutton)
- 1978: *Bridge to Terabithia* by Katherine Paterson (Crowell)

- 1977: *Roll of Thunder, Hear My Cry* by Mildred D. Taylor (Dial)
- 1976: *The Grey King* by Susan Cooper (McElderry/Atheneum)
- 1975: *M. C. Higgins, the Great* by Virginia Hamilton (Macmillan)
- 1974: *The Slave Dancer* by Paula Fox (Bradbury)
- 1973: *Julie of the Wolves* by Jean Craighead George (Harper)
- 1972: *Mrs. Frisby and the Rats of NIMH* by Robert C. O'Brien (Atheneum)
- 1971: *Summer of the Swans* by Betsy Byars (Viking)
- 1970: *Sounder* by William H. Armstrong (Harper)
- 1969: *The High King* by Lloyd Alexander (Holt)
- 1968: *From the Mixed-Up Files of Mrs. Basil E. Frankweiler* by E. L. Konigsburg (Atheneum)
- 1967: *Up a Road Slowly* by Irene Hunt (Follett)
- 1966: *I, Juan de Pareja* by Elizabeth Borton de Trevino (Farrar)
- 1965: *Shadow of a Bull* by Maia Wojciechowska (Atheneum)
- 1964: *It's Like This, Cat* by Emily Neville (Harper)
- 1963: *A Wrinkle in Time* by Madeleine L'Engle (Farrar)
- 1962: *The Bronze Bow* by Elizabeth George Speare (Houghton)
- 1961: *Island of the Blue Dolphins* by Scott O'Dell (Houghton)
- 1960: *Onion John* by Joseph Krumgold (Crowell)
- 1959: *The Witch of Blackbird Pond* by Elizabeth George Speare (Houghton)
- 1958: *Rifles for Watie* by Harold Keith (Crowell)
- 1957: *Miracles on Maple Hill* by Virginia Sorenson (Harcourt)
- 1956: *Carry On, Mr. Bowditch* by Jean Lee Latham (Houghton)
- 1955: *The Wheel on the School* by Meindert DeJong (Harper)
- 1954: *. . . And Now Miguel* by Joseph Krumgold (Crowell)
- 1953: *Secret of the Andes* by Ann Nolan Clark (Viking)
- 1952: *Ginger Pye* by Eleanor Estes (Harcourt)
- 1951: *Amos Fortune, Free Man* by Elizabeth Yates (Dutton)
- 1950: *The Door in the Wall* by Marguerite de Angeli (Doubleday)
- 1949: *King of the Wind* by Marguerite Henry (Rand McNally)
- 1948: *The Twenty-One Balloons* by William Pène du Bois (Viking)
- 1947: *Miss Hickory* by Carolyn Sherwin Bailey (Viking)
- 1946: *Strawberry Girl* by Lois Lenski (Lippincott)
- 1945: *Rabbit Hill* by Robert Lawson (Viking)
- 1944: *Johnny Tremain* by Esther Forbes (Houghton)
- 1943: *Adam of the Road* by Elizabeth Janet Gray (Viking)
- 1942: *The Matchlock Gun* by Walter Edmonds (Dodd)
- 1941: *Call It Courage* by Armstrong Sperry (Macmillan)
- 1940: *Daniel Boone* by James Daugherty (Viking)

- 1939: *Thimble Summer* by Elizabeth Enright (Rinehart)
- 1938: *The White Stag* by Kate Seredy (Viking)
- 1937: *Roller Skates* by Ruth Sawyer (Viking)
- 1936: *Caddie Woodlawn* by Carol Ryrie Brink (Macmillan)
- 1935: *Dobry* by Monica Shannon (Viking)
- 1934: *Invincible Louisa: The Story of the Author of* Little Women by Cornelia Meigs (Little, Brown)
- 1933: *Young Fu of the Upper Yangtze* by Elizabeth Lewis (Winston)
- 1932: *Waterless Mountain* by Laura Adams Armer (Longmans)
- 1931: *The Cat Who Went to Heaven* by Elizabeth Coatsworth (Macmillan)
- 1930: *Hitty, Her First Hundred Years* by Rachel Field (Macmillan)
- 1929: *The Trumpeter of Krakow* by Eric P. Kelly (Macmillan)
- 1928: *Gay Neck, the Story of a Pigeon* by Dhan Gopal Mukerji (Dutton)
- 1927: *Smoky, the Cowhorse* by Will James (Scribner)
- 1926: *Shen of the Sea* by Arthur Bowie Chrisman (Dutton)
- 1925: *Tales from Silver Lands* by Charles Finger (Doubleday)
- 1924: *The Dark Frigate* by Charles Hawes (Little, Brown)
- 1923: *The Voyages of Doctor Dolittle* by Hugh Lofting (Lippincott)
- 1922: *The Story of Mankind* by Hendrik Willem van Loon (Liveright)

For further information on the Newbery Medal Winners, check http://www.ala.org/ala/mgrps/divs/alsc/awardsgrants/bookmedia/newberymedal/newberywinners/medalwinners.cfm.

CALDECOTT MEDAL WINNERS

In conjunction with the John Newbery Awards for prestigious children's literature, the first Caldecott Medal was awarded to illustrator Dorothy P. Lathrop for *Animals of the Bible*, a picture book in 1938. This award is presented yearly to the artist creating the most distinguished American Picture Book for Children published in the United States. The medal is given in honor of Randolph Caldecott, a nineteenth-century English illustrator.

I have used many of the Caldecott books for my creative writing lessons over the years, at all grade levels, my favorite being Van Allsburg's *The Polar Express*, 1986.

I have also used these beautifully illustrated books with my students whose gifts are in the artistic arena of giftedness.

While I toyed with starting a Caldecott Club similar to our Newbery Club to award our school's gifted artists, I didn't . . . one of my regrets. However,

I hope this chapter spurs one or more of you creative parents and/or art educators reading this book to develop your own Caldecott Clubs for your school. Please let me know if you do. My heart will be happy!

For your convenience, I have included a listing of the Caldecott winners from 1938 to 2009.

ALSC: Caldecott Medal Winners 1938–2009:

- 2009: *The House in the Night*, illustrated by Beth Krommes, written by Susan Marie Swanson (Houghton Mifflin Company)
- 2008: *The Invention of Hugo Cabret* by Brian Selznick (Scholastic Press, an imprint of Scholastic)
- 2007: *Flotsam* by David Wiesner (Clarion)
- 2006: *The Hello, Goodbye Window*, illustrated by Chris Raschka and written by Norton Juster (Michael di Capua Books/Hyperion Books for Children)
- 2005: *Kitten's First Full Moon* by Kevin Henkes (Greenwillow Books/ Harper Collins Publishers)
- 2004: *The Man Who Walked Between the Towers* by Mordicai Gerstein (Roaring Brook Press/Millbrook Press)
- 2003: *My Friend Rabbit* by Eric Rohmann (Roaring Brook Press/Millbrook Press)
- 2002: *The Three Pigs* by David Wiesner (Clarion Publishers)
- 2001: *So You Want to be President* by Judith St. George (Philomel Publishers)
- 2000: *Joseph Had a Little Overcoat* by Simms Taback (Viking)
- 1999: *Snowflake Bentley*, illustrated by Mary Azarian; text by Jacqueline Briggs Martin (Houghton)
- 1998: *Rapunzel* by Paul O. Zelinsky (Dutton)
- 1997: *Golem* by David Wisniewski (Clarion)
- 1996: *Officer Buckle and Gloria* by Peggy Rathmann (Putnam)
- 1995: *Smoky Night*, illustrated by David Diaz; text by Eve Bunting (Harcourt)
- 1994: *Grandfather's Journey* by Allen Say; text edited by Walter Lorraine (Houghton)
- 1993: *Mirette on the High Wire* by Emily Arnold McCully (Putnam)
- 1992: *Tuesday* by David Wiesner (Clarion Books)
- 1991: *Black and White* by David Macaulay (Houghton)
- 1990: *Lon Po Po: A Red-Riding Hood Story from China* by Ed Young (Philomel)
- 1989: *Song and Dance Man*, illustrated by Stephen Gammell; text by Karen Ackerman (Knopf)

- 1988: *Owl Moon*, illustrated by John Schoenherr; text by Jane Yolen (Philomel)
- 1987: *Hey, Al*, illustrated by Richard Egielski; text by Arthur Yorinks (Farrar)
- 1986: *The Polar Express* by Chris Van Allsburg (Houghton)
- 1985: *Saint George and the Dragon*, illustrated by Trina Schart Hyman; text retold by Margaret Hodges (Little, Brown)
- 1984: *The Glorious Flight: Across the Channel with Louis Bleriot* by Alice & Martin Provensen (Viking)
- 1983: *Shadow*, translated and illustrated by Marcia Brown; original text in French by Blaise Cendrars (Scribner)
- 1982: *Jumanji* by Chris Van Allsburg (Houghton)
- 1981: *Fables* by Arnold Lobel (Harper)
- 1980: *Ox-Cart Man*, illustrated by Barbara Cooney; text by Donald Hall (Viking)
- 1979: *The Girl Who Loved Wild Horses* by Paul Goble (Bradbury)
- 1978: *Noah's Ark* by Peter Spier (Doubleday)
- 1977: *Ashanti to Zulu: African Traditions*, illustrated by Leo & Diane Dillon; text by Margaret Musgrove (Dial)
- 1976: *Why Mosquitoes Buzz in People's Ears*, illustrated by Leo & Diane Dillon; text retold by Verna Aardema (Dial)
- 1975: *Arrow to the Sun* by Gerald McDermott (Viking)
- 1974: *Duffy and the Devil*, illustrated by Margot Zemach; retold by Harve Zemach (Farrar)
- 1973: *The Funny Little Woman*, illustrated by Blair Lent; text retold by Arlene Mosel (Dutton)
- 1972: *One Fine Day*, retold and illustrated by Nonny Hogrogian (Macmillan)
- 1971: *A Story A Story*, retold and illustrated by Gail E. Haley (Atheneum)
- 1970: *Sylvester and the Magic Pebble* by William Steig (Windmill Books)
- 1969: *The Fool of the World and the Flying Ship*, illustrated by Uri Shulevitz; text retold by Arthur Ransome (Farrar)
- 1968: *Drummer Hoff*, illustrated by Ed Emberley; text adapted by Barbara Emberley (Prentice-Hall)
- 1967: *Sam, Bangs & Moonshine* by Evaline Ness (Holt)
- 1966: *Always Room for One More*, illustrated by Nonny Hogrogian; text by Sorche Nic Leodhas, pseud. [Leclair Alger] (Holt)
- 1965: *May I Bring a Friend?* illustrated by Beni Montresor; text by Beatrice Schenk de Regniers (Atheneum)
- 1964: *Where the Wild Things Are* by Maurice Sendak (Harper)
- 1963: *The Snowy Day* by Ezra Jack Keats (Viking)

- 1962: *Once a Mouse*, retold and illustrated by Marcia Brown (Scribner)
- 1961: *Baboushka and the Three Kings*, illustrated by Nicolas Sidjakov; text by Ruth Robbins (Parnassus)
- 1960: *Nine Days to Christmas*, illustrated by Marie Hall Ets; text by Marie Hall Ets and Aurora Labastida (Viking)
- 1959: *Chanticleer and the Fox*, illustrated by Barbara Cooney; text adapted from Chaucer's Canterbury Tales by Barbara Cooney (Crowell)
- 1958: *Time of Wonder* by Robert McCloskey (Viking)
- 1957: *A Tree Is Nice*, illustrated by Marc Simont; text by Janice Udry (Harper)
- 1956: *Frog Went A-Courtin'*, illustrated by Feodor Rojankovsky; text retold by John Langstaff (Harcourt)
- 1955: *Cinderella, or the Little Glass Slipper*, illustrated by Marcia Brown; text translated from Charles Perrault by Marcia Brown (Scribner)
- 1954: *Madeline's Rescue* by Ludwig Bemelmans (Viking)
- 1953: *The Biggest Bear* by Lynd Ward (Houghton)
- 1952: *Finders Keepers*, illustrated by Nicolas, pseud. (Nicholas Mordvinoff); text by Will, pseud. [William Lipkind] (Harcourt)
- 1951: *The Egg Tree* by Katherine Milhous (Scribner)
- 1950: *Song of the Swallows* by Leo Politi (Scribner)
- 1949: *The Big Snow* by Berta & Elmer Hader (Macmillan)
- 1948: *White Snow, Bright Snow*, illustrated by Roger Duvoisin; text by Alvin Tresselt (Lothrop)
- 1947: *The Little Island*, illustrated by Leonard Weisgard; text by Golden MacDonald, pseud. [Margaret Wise Brown] (Doubleday)
- 1946: *The Rooster Crows* by Maude & Miska Petersham (Macmillan)
- 1945: *Prayer for a Child*, illustrated by Elizabeth Orton Jones; text by Rachel Field (Macmillan)
- 1944: *Many Moons*, illustrated by Louis Slobodkin; text by James Thurber (Harcourt)
- 1943: *The Little House* by Virginia Lee Burton (Houghton)
- 1942: *Make Way for Ducklings* by Robert McCloskey (Viking)
- 1941: *They Were Strong and Good*, by Robert Lawson (Viking)
- 1940: *Abraham Lincoln* by Ingri & Edgar Parin d'Aulaire (Doubleday)
- 1939: *Mei Li* by Thomas Handforth (Doubleday)
- 1938: *Animals of the Bible, A Picture Book*, illustrated by Dorothy P. Lathrop; text selected by Helen Dean Fish (Lippincott)

You may also access more information about the Caldecotts and Newberys at www.ala.org/alsc/nquick.html or www.ala.org/ala/mgrps/divs/alsc/awards-grants/bookmedia/caldecottmedal/caldecotthonors/caldecottmedal.cfm.

Art opens up the magic of the mind.

—Gribb

Q. I have three very precocious and gifted children ages seven, ten, and twelve. All were reading fluently before entering public schools and continue to have a love for reading. Can you suggest any books where the primary character(s) are gifted? I'd like to encourage my children through gifted heroes/heroines as role models in literature.

A. Yes! I certainly have my favorite: The *Anne of Green Gables* series. Not only was Anne spunky, bright, gifted, and mischievous (in a good sort of way, of course), she was also a redhead like myself. I was in my glory reading L. M. Montgomery's books. Eventually, I started asking my graduate students who their favorite gifted characters in a book were. Following is a list of the more popular book titles they suggested, whose protagonists were gifted in one or more areas.

Q. What do you recommend as excellent literature for gifted teenagers? Both our sons are being "turned off" by the required readings in high school and are quickly losing their lifelong love of reading!

A. I will never forget my reaction while reading Bach's *Jonathan Livingston Seagull*, when the flock stoned Jonathan to death while he tried to share the incredible feat of breaking the sound barrier! In retrospect, what a good lesson to learn about society's perpetual rejection of brilliance, achievement, and change!

I asked my students what their favorite book was as a teenager. I have compiled the more popular titles for you. I think your sons will find much of the readings from these lists exciting and thought provoking.

P.S. I've also included a list of Favorite Children's Books for parents of younger children.

Reflecting the policy goals of the New York State Board of Regents (1995) are the Regents Bill of Rights for Children desired for all of New York State's children. Notice Goal 4: *Each child has the right to an education appropriate for his or her individual needs.*

Bravo! Does this include gifted children being serviced at their aptitude levels? This is a wonderful concept for all children and a dream of mine in this lifetime!

• All children have the right to a healthy, secure nurturing infancy and early childhood.
• All children have the right to live in circumstances that permit healthy intellectual, emotional, physical, and moral development.

Table 2.2. Favorite Books with a Gifted Primary Character

Author	Title	Copyright	Publisher
Bemelmans, Ludwig	Madeline	1976	Viking Penguin
Benezia, Mike	Picasso	1988	Regensteiner Publishing Enterprises, Inc.
Brighton, Catherine	The Fossil Girl	1999	Millbrook Press
Bush, Timothy	Grant! The Primitive Core Boy	1995	Random House Books
Cade Bambara, Toni	Raymonds Run	1993	The Creative Company
Carmody, Isobelle	Obernewtyn	1987	Puffin Books
Caswell, Brian	A Cage of Butterflies	1992	University of Queensland Press
Chesworth, Michael	Archibald Frisby	1994	Farrar Straus & Giroux
Cleary, Beverly	Romona the Brave	1975	Dell Publishing, Co., Inc.
Clements, Andrew	The Landry News	1999	Aladdin Paperbacks
Cohen, Barbara	213 Valentines	1991	Henry-Holt and Co.
Cooper, Susan	The Dark Is Rising	1973	Collies Books
Dahls, Ronald	Charlie and the Chocolate Factory	1964	Alfred Knopf, Inc.
Dean Myers, Walter	Darnell Rock Reporting	1994	Bantam Doubleday Dell Books for Young Readers
Ericsson Lindgren, Astrid	Pippi Longstocking	1976	Penguin Putnam Books for Young Readers
Estes, Eleanor	The Hundred Dresses	1944/1973	Scholastic, Inc.
Fleischman, Paul	Weslandia	1999	Candlewick Press
Forbes, Esther	Johnny Tremain	1943	Bantam Double Day Dell for Young Readers
Galdone, Paul	The Little Red Hen	1991	Houghton Mifflin, Co.
Hinton, S. E.	The Outsiders	1997	Viking Penguin
Hodgson Burnett, Frances	A Little Princess	1981	Watermill Press
Hoffmann, Mary	Amazing Grace	1991	Kirkus Associates
Ingalls Wilder, Laura	Little Town in the Big Woods	1976	HarperCollins Children's Books
Jacques, Brian	Redwall	1986	Random House
Kallok, Emma	The Diary of Chickabiddy Baby	1999	Scholastic
King- Smith, Dick	A Mouse Called Wolf	1977	Dell Yearling

(continued)

Table 2.2. (continued)

Author	Title	Copyright	Publisher
Klein	Halfway Across the Galaxy and Turn Left	1985	Puffin Books
Konigsburg, E. L.	The View from Saturday	1996	Aladdin Paperbacks
Lackey, Mercedes	Magic's Pawn	1990	Daw Books
LeGuin, Ursula	The Earthsea Quartet	1993	Puffin Books
L'Engle, Madeleine	A Ring of Endless Light	1981	Bantam Doubleday Books
Lowry, Lois	Anastasia Krupnik	1981	Bantam Doubleday Dell Publishing Group
Lowry, Lois	The Giver	1993	Bantam Doubleday Dell Books
McLerran, Alice	Roxaboxen	1991	William Morrow & Co.
Montague, Jeanne	Midnight Moon	1985	St. Martin Press
Montgomery, L. M.	Anne of Green Gables	1972	Bantam Books, Incorporated
Moon, Nicole	Lucy's Picture	1995	Dial Books
Nostlinger, Christine	Konrad	1976	Andersen Press Limited
Odgers, Sally	Translations in Celadon	1998	Harper Collins
Parish, Peggy	Amelia Bedelia		Scholastic Book Services
Potok, Chaim	The Chosen	1976	Fawcett Book Group
Rachlin, Ann	Mozart	1992	Barron's Educational Services
Richter, Conrad	The Light in the Forest	1994	Random House, Inc.
Rowling, J. K.	Harry Potter and the Sorcerer's Stone	1998	Scholastic Trade
Rowling, J.K.	Harry Potter and the Goblet of Fire	2000	Scholastic Press
Salinger, D. L.	The Catcher in the Rye	1991	Little, Brown and Company
Scierzka, Jan	The True Story of the Three Little Pigs	1996	Penguin Putnam Books for Young Readers
Spinelli, Jerry	Maniac Magee	1990	Little Brown and Company
Stewart, Sara	The Gardner	1997	Harper-Collins Canada Ltd.
Sullivan, Anne, and Helen Keller	Helen Keller	1989	Scholastic
Tusa, Tricia	Bunnies in My Head	1998	University of Texas M.D. Anderson Cancer Ctr.
White, E. B.	Charlotte Webb	1980	Harper Collens
Willimas Bianco, Margery	Velveteen Rabbit	1988	Random House, Inc.
Wise Brown, Margret	Runaway Bunny	1942	Harper Trophey, Collins
Wynne Jones, Diana	Charmed Life	1989	Morrow, William & Co
Wynne Jones, Diana	The Lives of Christopher Chant	1988	Methuen

Table 2.3. Favorite Teenage Books

Author	Title	Year	Publisher
Atwood, Margaret	The Handmaid's Tale	1998	Vintage Anchor Publishing
Bach, Richard	Jonathan Livingston Seagull	1973	Mass Market Paperback
Blume, Judy	Are You There God? It's Me Margaret	1970	Simon & Schuster Children's Publishing Division
Blume, Judy	Blubber	1976	Bantam Double Day Dell Books
Brown, Claude	Manchild in the Promise Land	1999	Simon & Schuster
Bryant, Bonnie	The Horse Whisperer	1998	Bantam Books
Burnford, Sheila	The Incredible Journey	1996	Bantam Doubleday Dell Books for Young Readers
Carmichael, Stokely S., With Charles V. Hamilton	Black Power	1976	Vintage Books
Chopin, Kate	The Awakening	1981	Bantam Books
Crane, Stephen	Red Badge of Courage	1990	Doherty, Tom Associates, LLC
Dickens, Charles	Great Expectations	1990	Double Day Dell
Downing Hahn, Mary	Daphne's Book	1983	Bantum Skylark Books
Fanon, Frantz	White Skin Black Mask	1976	Grove/Atlantic, Inc.
Haley, Alex	Malcolm "X"	1975	Random House
James, George G. M.	Stolen Legacy	1997	Yale University Press
Keene, Carolyn	The Bungalow Mystery	1960	Grosse & Dunlap
King, Stephen	The Stand	1978	Doubleday
Konigsburg, E. L.	From the Mixed-up Files of Mrs. Basil E. Frankweiler	1967	Simon & Schuster
Lamb, Wally	She's Come Undone	1998	Pocket Books
Lee, Harper	To Kill a Mockingbird	1988	Warner Books
Lowry, Lois	The Giver	1994	
Martin, Ann M.	The Baby-sitters Club	1986	Scholastic
Miller, Arthur	The Crucible	1952	Dramatists Play Service, Incorporated
Mitchel, Margaret	Gone with the Wind	1936	McMillan
O'Brien, Tim	The Things They Carried	1998	Random House, Incorporated

(continued)

Table 2.3. *(continued)*

Author	Title	Year	Publisher
Paterson, Katherine	*Bridge to Terabithia*	1977	Harper Collins
Paulsen, Gary	*Hatchet*	1987	Penguin Group
Petersen Haddix, Margaret	*Among the Hidden*	2000	Simon & Schuster
Quinlen, Anna	*Black and Blue*	1998	Random House
Rand, Ayn	*Atlas Shrugged*	1996	Mass Market Paperback
Rand, Ayn	*The Fountainhead*	1952	Signet (Penquin Books)
Rawls, Wilson	*Where the Red Fern Grows*	1961	Bantam Books
Rockwell, Thomas	*How to Eat Fried Worms*	1973	Franklin Watts
Sachar, Louis	*Holes*	1999	Scholastic
Salinger, J. D.	*Catcher in the Rye*	1991	Little, Brown and Company
Shelley, Mary	*Frankenstein*	1994	Norton, W. W. & Company, Inc.
Simon, Neil	*Biloxi Blues*	1986	Random House
Skene Catling, Patrick	*The Chocolate Touch*	1976	Bantam Book
Spinelli, Jerry	*Maniac Magee*	1991	Harper Collins
Spinelli, Jerry	*Wringer*	1997	Harper Collins
Steinbeck, John	*Of Mice and Men*	1937	Bantam Book
Steinbeck, John	*The Pearl*	1968	The Viking Press
Taylor, Mildred D.	*Roll of Thunder, Hear My Cry*	1976	Dial Books
Uris, Leon	*Exodus*	1958	Doubleday & Company
Wiesel, Elie	*Night*	1982	Bantam Doubleday Dell Publishing Group

Table 2.4. Favorite Children's Books

Author	Title	Year	Publisher
Adler, David A.	Cam Jansen and the Missing Cookie	1996	Viking
Berenstain, Stan and Jan	All of the Bernstein Bears Books	1980s	Random House
Blume, Judy	Are You There, God? It's Me Margaret	1971	Bantam Doubleday Dell Publishing Group
Blume, Judy	Superfudge	1977	Harcourt Brace
Brittain, Bill	All the Money in the World	1979	Harper Row Junior Books
Burnford, Sheila	The Incredible Journey	1996	Laureleaf
Burton, Virginia Lee	Mike Mulligan and His Steam Shovel	1939	Houghton Mifflin Co.
Caswell, Brian	A Cage of Butterflies	1992	University of Queensland Press
Craighead George, Jean	Julie of the Wolves	1987	Hapercollins Juvenile Books
Cutts & Sliverstein	The House that Jack Built	1979	Troll Associates
Dahl, Ronald	Charlie and the Chocolate Factory	1998	Puffin
Dahl, Ronald	The BFG	1982	Penguin Group
Dann, Max	Ernest Pickles Remarkable Robot	1984	Oxford University Press
Dr. Seuss	The Cat in the Hat	1976	Random House
Dr. Seuss	The Lorax	1976	Random House
Erdrich, Louise	The Birchbark House	1999	Hyperion Press
Fitzgerald, John D.	The Great Brain	1972	Yearling Books
Fitzhugh, Louise	Harriet The Spy	2000	Bantam
Fox, Mem	Wilfred Gordon McDonald Partridge	1984	Kane/Miller Book Pub.
George Speare, Elizabeth	The Witch of Blackbird Pond	1958	Houghton Mifflin Co.
Gramatky, Hardie	Little Toot	1939	G.P. Putnam's Sons
Juster, Norton	The Phantom Tollbooth	1988	Random House
Konigsburg, E. L.	From the Mixed-Up Files of Mrs. Basil E. Frankeweiler	1970	Atheneum School & Library Bindling
Le Tord, Bijou	A Blue Butterfly ; A Story about Claude Monet	1995	Delacorte Press
L'Engle, Madeleine	A Wrinkle in Time	1962	Farrar Straus Giroux
Littledale, Freya	The Magic Fish	1966/1985	Scholastic, Inc.
Lobel, Arnold	Frog and Toad Are Friends	1970	Harper & Row

(continued)

Table 2.4. *(continued)*

Author	Title	Year	Publisher
Lobel, Arnold	Frog and Toad Together	1979	HarperCollins Children's Books
London, Jack	Call of the Wild	1990	Tor Books
Manus Pinkwater, Daniel	5 Novels: Alan Mendelsohn the Boy from Mars, Slaves of Speigel, the Snarkout Boys and the Avocado of Deathe, the Last Guru, Young Adult Novel	1997	Farrar Straus & Giroux
Mayer, Mercer	Just Grandma and Me	1983	Golden Books
Munsch, Robert N., and Michael	The Paper Bag Princess	1985	Firefly Books LTD
Norton, Mary	The Borrowers	1998	Harcourt Brace
O'Brien, Robert C.	Mrs. Frisby and the Rats of Nimh	1974	Atheneum
O'Dell, Scott	Island of the Blue Dolphins	1990	Hougton Mifflin
Ottley, Ted	Code of Deception	1993	Random House, Australia
Paulsen, Gary	M.C. Higgins, the Great	1999	Simon & Schuster
Paulson, Gary	Hatchet	1999	Aladdin
Pullman, Philip	The Golden Compass His Dark Materials, No. 1	1996	Knopf
Rawls, Wilson	Where the Red Fern Grows	1961	Curtis Publishing Company
Reid Banks, Lynne	The Indian in the Cupboard	1982	Morrow William & Company
Roald, Dahl	James and the Giant Peach	1961	Penguine Books
Rowling, J. K.	Harry Potter and the Goblet of Fire	2000	Scholastic Press
Rowling, J. K.	Harry Potter and the Sorcerer's Stone	1998	Scholastic Trade
Sachar, Louis	Holes	1998	Farrar Straus & Giroux
Selden, George	The Cricket in Times Square	1983	Farrar Straus & Giroux
Shannon, David	A Bad Case of The Stripes	1988	Blue Sky Press
Steig, William	Dominic	1984	Farrar Straus & Giroux
Taylor, Mildred D.	Roll of Thunder, Hear My Cry	1997	Puffin
Tolan, Stephanie S.	Welcome to the Ark	1996	Morrow
Van Allsburg, Chris	The Polar Express	1985	Scholastic
White, E. B.	Charlotte's Web	1987	Harper Collins
Williams, Margery	Velveteen Rabbit	1922/1991	Delcaurte Press
Wise Brown, Margaret	Goodnight Moon	1947/1975	Harper & Row

- All children have the right to a free, sound basic education.
- Each child has the right to an education appropriate for his or her individual needs.
- All children have the right to an education that respects their culture, race, socioeconomic background, and the language of their home.
- All children have the right to schools and educational programs that are effective.
- All children have the right to educational programs that prepare them for jobs, college, for responsible family life, and for citizenship in a self-governing society.
- All children have the right to pursue their education without fear.
- All children have the right to the resources needed to secure their educational rights.
- All children are entitled to an education, which involves responsibilities as well as rights.

Adopted from Gems of AGATE: Advocacy for Gifted and Talented Education in New York State, 1995.

Chapter Three

Perfectionism and
Social Emotional Development

I am a recovering perfectionist. It's true. I can laugh saying it now, but I spent a great many of my younger years suffering with the pain of perfectionism, and it was painful!

I can clearly remember the Sunday I was playing "Toccata and Fugue in F Minor."

I was twelve years old and organist at the First Presbyterian Church in Medina, New York. I made a chord mistake and spent the afternoon crying on my bed because I was such a failure in my own mind and heart. Every single week I prepared the organ music for the Sunday services. All this was done between the ages of twelve and eighteen. Can you imagine? I thought I was a failure because I would make an occasional playing error. Now I wonder how I could even assume that much responsibility at such a young and vulnerable age.

Gifted children often have the talents and responsibilities to assume more adult roles. They are often multipotential. These precious youngsters need guidance with perfectionism, making appropriate choices, and managing their time.

The NAGC Standards pose five guiding questions to reflect upon your effective socio-emotional guidance and counseling practices and which I encourage you to keep in mind as you help and support your gifted children.

- How do gifted students benefit from having access to a counselor who is familiar with the characteristics and socio-emotional needs of gifted learners?
- What are the components of effective career counseling for gifted students? How is this different from what is traditionally offered to students in middle and high school?

- Why is it important to specifically identify and address the needs of gifted at-risk learners in gifted education program planning?
- What skills do you think are needed by gifted learners that will enable them "to be their own best advocate" for high-quality educational experiences? Does this skill set differ depending on the age of the child?
- How might you respond to a gifted student who is underachieving in your classroom?

Q. Can you explain to me just who perfectionists are?

A. Sure. Generally, perfectionists are people who are very bright and have succeeded because of their high intelligence and/or talents. They often can see many solutions to one problem and an infinite number of ways to solve it. They can create and not feel comfortable with a "finishing point," always knowing more "could be done." Many times, perfectionists will avoid new experiences, due to a fear of failure. They're afraid others will view them as inadequate.

Perfectionists have exceedingly high expectations—for themselves and others. On a personal level, these can lead to a workaholic syndrome. On a social level, personality conflicts can ensue at work and at home.

Children can learn perfectionism from their parents and their interactions with them. Such children measure parental acceptance by their perfect deeds and avoid areas where mistakes might be made and a loss of love might occur.

With proper counseling, perfectionists can be helped to lead a more balanced and realistic lifestyle. I'm not sure there is a complete cure for perfectionism, but recovery is possible.

Q. Most parents would probably want this problem, but I'm not sure it's healthy. Our eleven-year-old gifted son is a straight A student, top in his class academically, involved on the soccer team, and plays first chair violin in the orchestra. The problem is, Jonathan is so conscientious, he studies/practices all the time, to the exclusion of joining us on family outings, picnics, sports games, or any other form of entertainment. We're very proud of his accomplishments, but somehow, I just don't think this behavior is normal nor healthy. Is it?

A. You're right on one count, not on the other. This behavior is normal for a severe perfectionist and can lead to serious emotional and/or physical consequences if allowed to continue over a long period of time. You're quite right that this behavior is not healthy.

You can and need to start intervening to help Jonathan with the following steps:

Figure 3.1. No, Tommy, you won't fail.

1. Use the time management sheets at the end of chapter 4—"Time Management, Homework Issues and SRS." Plan out times throughout the week and month that your son *will* join with you in planned family events. The type and choice of outing can be his, allowing freedom and flexibility. This can certainly include watching some favorite TV shows or movies together or quiet reading time.
2. Plan regular times to sit and talk with Jonathan. Gifted children have a multitude of ideas and thoughts going on in their heads and they benefit greatly by talking, helping keep a stable and normal balance.
3. Either utilize the services of your school's counselor or a private one of your choice for Jonathan to speak with. Many times a child is much more likely to speak with a trusted professional than with a family member or favorite teacher.
4. Walk together. Walking is a wonderful stress reducer, helping build up natural endorphins in the brain and a super jibber-jabber time. Once you

get your son beyond the initial resistance to the idea, he'll actually look forward to the time together.

5. Always let your son know you care about him. Phrases of endearment and daily hugs/touches provide an immediate and important strength and balance to one's day. Try any or all of these suggestions. I would be very surprised if you didn't notice improvement after just one or two weeks. If not, give me a call or e-mail for additional activities.

Q. Our gifted thirteen-year-old daughter is so conscientious and focused on achieving straight As in school, we can't even get her to join us on family outings nor any other social situations. We appreciate her determination to succeed in school academically, but is this normal?

A. Yes and no. Yes, for severe perfectionists; no, for balanced and healthy children. I don't mean to scare you, but you do need to intercede now with your daughter's one-sided behavior—academics to the exclusion of social and family activities. The longer this behavior is allowed to go on, the harder it will be to bring your daughter to a more balanced lifestyle. Perfectionism is a painful behavior. Good is never good enough; excellence is never excellent enough. There can be many reasons for her perfectionism.

Regardless of your daughter's reason(s), it is interfering with her social and family life and counseling now would help her a great deal. One option is counseling within school, although this is many times embarrassing to the children among their peers. Unfortunately, often the school counselor's/psychologist's time is overloaded with the low-achieving and discipline students.

There might be subsidized family counseling centers through your local township and/or hospitals.

Private psychologists and counselors could be costly, but are often covered by medical health insurance companies.

Check with your daughter's teacher(s) or call your school psychologist to find the names of the professionals who specialize in gifted children and/or severe perfectionists. The sooner you start on this road, the better.

Q. Why are some students "workaholics?"

A. The "healthy" reason is that these children want to succeed, produce excellence in their work, and keep up with the homework demands of their schools and teachers . . . all honorable goals.

However, all too often, workaholic children are that way due to a variety of factors, which do not constitute a balanced, healthy emotional lifestyle. Children most at risk for becoming workaholics are those between the ages of six and twelve who have repeatedly been rewarded only for the things they do rather than for the personal qualities they have.

Figure 3.2. AP social studies.

Many times, these children have parents who push them to extreme and are very dominant in their children's development. Such parents often are trying to live and succeed through their gifted children. More often than not, these children "burn out" as adults and never even come close to achieving their true potential.

Perfection, and its many roles, also plays a very strong factor in producing severe workaholics. Adderholdt and Goldberg aptly describe the eight games perfectionists play, believing that achievement and self-worth are one and the same (1999, 18–21):[1]

- *Riding the Mood Roller Coaster*
  You set a goal for yourself (for example: to ace a math test). You do it—and you feel great!

  But you don't ace the next one—you get an 89. And you feel awful. Your friends and family notice and try to reassure you, but you're prickly and irritable and suspicious of their motives. Why would they praise you? You're not worth it; you couldn't even get that A you were after!

  Then along comes the next math test, you ace it, and you're riding high again. It's exhausting! You feel excited and capable when you do well, and unacceptable and ashamed when you don't.

- *The Numbers Game*
  The quantity of achievements or actions becomes more important than the quality. You start to focus on how many trophies you win, papers you write, awards you receive, honors you reap—not what you're learning or what they're really worth. No number is ever high enough; you just keep counting.
- *Focusing on the Future*
  You give an especially brilliant speech during the debate. Everybody comes up afterward and tells you that you were inspiring. But all you can think about is what you forgot to say. Or your mind is already on next week's essay contest—what if you don't outdo yourself in that, too?

  Don't even try to sit back and savor your success; that's not what perfectionists do. There's no time—not when you're already planning the future and worrying about the things you must do to succeed.
- *Pining over the Past*
  "If only I'd . . ." "Why didn't I . . ." "This wouldn't have happened if I'd started sooner . . ." "If I'd put down that answer, I would've got an A instead of a B." You don't let things go. You chew on them relentlessly, like a dog gnawing on a bone. Thoughts like these keep you stuck in the same old groove of the same old record.
- *Telescopic Thinking*
  You use both ends of a telescope when viewing your achievements. When looking at the goals you haven't met, you use the magnifying end so they appear much larger than they really are. But when looking at those you have met, you use the "minifying" end so they appear minute and insignificant.

  For example, you win the district tennis match, but you can't feel good about it because you haven't won the state. Or you compete in the state tournament, making it all the way to the championship match, but feel outclassed the minute your opponent pulls ahead.
- *Putting Your Goals First*
  Given a choice between sleeping and studying, you study—even if it means drinking gallons of coffee or taking caffeine pills, pinching yourself to stay awake, and making yourself sick. Or given the choice between going out with friends or working on your volleyball serve, you opt for the gym. Your achievement goals always come before fun or friends or your own good health.
- *Getting It Right*
  You're not satisfied with anything but the best, most perfect results, so you do the same thing again . . . and again . . . and again until you get it right. Maybe you repeat the same course in school until you get the A you're determined to have. Or you play the same piece of music over and over and over and over and over and over. And over and over and over and over and over

again, hating yourself because you're so slow. You're worried that others will know how hard you worked when you want it to appear effortless.

• *All-or-Nothing Thinking*

You're not satisfied unless you have it all—all the track trophies, all the academic awards your school can give, all the leadership positions in your clubs. One B or one second place is enough to tip you over into the feeling that you've failed, that you're not good enough.

As school counselors and educators become more aware of perfectionism and how it adversely affects so many of our gifted children, proactive counseling classes and interventions will hopefully become a more standard part of our children's days.

Q. Year after year after year, teachers and counselors have told my husband and me that our son is an underachiever, yet none of the teachers have been able to get him to "achieve" at their "expected levels" for him. He maintains a B average, plays sports, and seems pretty content to us. Should we be expecting more of him? We want our son to be happy, healthy, and psychologically adjusted. Are we letting him "waste his potential?"

A. It sounds to me like you're doing just fine in your parenting role. Many perfectionist-gifted children are emotionally devastated if they earn a grade of B, yet, by definition, a B represents an achievement which is "very good!"

I do have to wonder if your son is achieving Bs because he already knows the grade level material(s) and can breeze right through the assignments and tests. I am also concerned that he might be an underachiever because he is

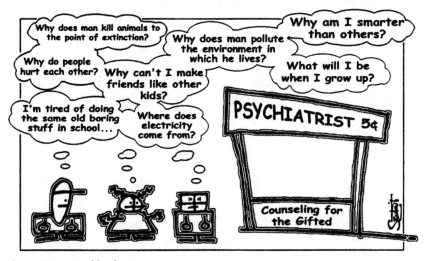

Figure 3.3. Psychiatrist 5¢.

not being educated at his aptitude level, like so many of our gifted children in American schools. If this is the case, I encourage you to meet with your son's teachers and review his achievement and nationally normed scores. If his test scores indicate he has been and/or is achieving one, two, or even more years ahead of his peers and grade-level expectations, then I suspect this is why the teachers have been suggesting "underachievement" to you.

Be careful with the solution(s) suggested. Many times, gifted children are given more work as a challenge and this becomes the "typical punishment" for being bright! Enrichment is also overused to the point that the overload of enrichment activities at grade levels can be seen coming out of the students' ears!

At the elementary level, compacting is a wonderful solution to testing children through materials they already know and getting them educated at an instructional level compatible to their achievement and aptitude. This is the positive. The negative is oftentimes high-achieving students are given packets to work on at a higher-grade level, but without proper instructions and monitoring. They are often left to sit in the hall outside the room to do their assignment(s). This is a lonely road to walk for these students and not educationally instructive nor emotionally supportive.

In middle and high schools, accelerated courses and/or AP courses often serve to educate the gifted and more cognitively advanced students. The positive is that high-achieving students are together and hopefully working at compatible aptitude levels. The negatives could be excessive amounts of homework and in some districts, AP courses are not weighted, so an A in advanced calculus is weighted the same as an A in regular calculus. Cumulative averages remain the same, yet amount and degree of work vary significantly. Class standings could be affected as well as scholarship awards.

These are ideas to consider when you meet with your son's teacher(s) and review his test scores and patterns of achievement.

If you do agree that advancing his studies is an appropriate answer, make sure you include your son in on the discussion. Depending on how long he has been underachieving, if this is the case, working at the appropriate aptitudinal level more than likely is going to be a jolt, both academically and emotionally.

First and foremost, your son's emotional and physical health are important. Right now it sounds like he's pretty happy and successful according to basic school standards and so are you. Working together with your son and his teachers, I suspect you'll come up with the proper answer and I'm only a phone call away if you find yourself in a dilemma.

Q. My nine-year-old son will lie awake for hours each night, unable to fall asleep. Is there anything I can do to help him gain a more peaceful night's sleep? Suggestions, please.

Figure 3.4. How is Miss Brain today?

A. When I first started teaching my "Parenting of Gifted" class at a local university, it rapidly became very clear that many of the parents had children who could not sleep well. My answer to them was, talk, talk, talk! In fact, I promised that if each parent sat on his or her child's bed and talked with his or her child for the next seven nights, there would be no more "sleep" problems. I promised.

What were they to talk about? Anything . . . I suggested letting the children lead the conversation(s). Mrs. P reported her son talked three hours the first night, from 10 p.m. to 1 a.m. She even dozed off in the rocking chair a few times but her son simply awakened her. Progress? . . . . yes! By the fifth night Roger was dozing off to a peaceful sleep after forty-five minutes of talking and Mr. P traded some nights with Mrs. P, so she could have a full night of sleep herself!

Twelve of the fifteen parents reported positive progress with their children's sleep patterns at our next class.

Q. How can I get counseling help at school for my gifted nine-year-old? He has trouble relating to his peers and is a severe perfectionist. The counseling time allotted to our school is being used up by the slower-achieving students, special education students, and/or troublemakers. We can't afford to pay for outside counseling services.

A. I literally had to fight ten years to get any counseling time whatsoever for the children in my self-contained gifted classroom, and then it was only for thirty minutes a week! Gifted students have unique counseling needs, including social/emotional adjustment, perfectionism, career planning, underachievement, multipotentiality, and family relationships. First, talk to your child's teachers in gaining support for in-school counseling. Second, check your child's group IQ test results and standardized achievement test scores, or you can request an individual WISQ-R by the school psychologist. This score usually runs higher than the group normed tests. This gives you positive "data" as you request a fair and appropriate education for your child, including counseling.

A note from your child's pediatrician requesting testing and/or counseling is usually beneficial as well.

If all else fails, then go to your administration and school board representative(s)—but always in a positive and supportive role. I know it's very frustrating at times, but keep P and P—positive and proactive.

Q. My teenage daughter seems to be crying at the slightest little happening at home. She argues constantly with her father and me, as well as her two younger siblings, and is sleeping much more than usual. Her grades are starting to drop and I'm beginning to seriously worry about her. Could she be depressed or just going through the "struggles" of teenage years? Susan is fifteen years old.

A. Many times there is a fine line between the symptoms of excessive stress, "teenage turmoil," and depression. There is a clear difference with clinical depression. This needs to be treated by a trained professional. Susan cannot just "will" her way out of clinical depression. The fact that your daughter is sleeping excessively and crying with little provocation suggests to me an immediate visit to her internist. He or she can provide a proper diagnosis and the necessary medication, if Susan is clinically depressed.

If not, Susan still needs help dealing with the events going on in her life. So many of today's gifted children are multipotential and have excessively overloaded schedules and commitments, pursuing excellence in many of their gifted areas.

Multipotential high school children are often involved in AP classes, musical groups, debate clubs, church groups, athletics, community services, and mentorships. This list goes on and on and on! Coupled with an office visit to Susan's internist, please take the time to sit down with her and talk. She may be initially resistant, but after a burst of tears, she may well start blurting out the major cause of her changes in behavior, including being overwhelmed with too many activities. She may also need help with time management and study habits, which I cover in another chapter.

The main thrust here is to get started with an intervention.

Q. What happens to gifted children? Do most succeed as adults?

A. Certainly giftedness is not a sole measure of success in life. There are a variety of variables which can and do affect a gifted child's success as an adult. Overall, I agree with Ellen Winner's summation of the factors that predict the four possible combinations of "gifted child and adult outcomes" (1996):

- Those gifted children most likely to develop their talent to the level of an expert will be those who have high drive and the ability to focus and derive flow from their work; those who grow up in families that combine stimulation with support; and those who are fortunate to have inspiring teachers, mentors, and role models.
- Those gifted children most likely to leave their creative mark on a domain in adulthood will also have high drive, focus and flow, and inspiring mentors and models. But in two other areas they should be different. They should be willing to be nonconforming, take risks, and shake up the established tradition. And they should be more likely than those who become experts to have grown up in stressful family conditions. (While stress may be a facilitating factor, it is surely not sufficient, and is not a factor for parents to strive for!) Many are also likely to develop some form of affective disorder. In addition, they must be born when the times are right: their domains must be ready for the kinds of changes they envision, and there must not be too many others likely to beat them in revolutionizing the domain first.

- Those gifted children predicted to burn out are those whose parents push them to extremes and are overinvolved in their development. These parents differ from those who produce creative children. Parents of future creators cause stress in their children's lives, but they are not overinvolved. Instead, they encourage independence in their offspring. But the difficulty of prediction is brought home by the fact that John Stuart Mill, who was excessively pushed by his father, did not drop out, whereas William James Sidis did.
- Those gifted children not "born into" a domain often discover their ultimate calling in adulthood when they are catalyzed by a crystallizing experience—a life-changing event in which a gift is discovered and self-doubts are dispelled.

I personally have always fallen into the category of "should be willing to be nonconforming, take risks, and shake up the established tradition!" This was never a conscious decision nor easy path to follow. I was always personally and professionally true to myself and ideals. It seemed to me to be the only way to go!

I have become increasingly aware of the need to support, guide, and direct our nonconforming, risk-taking gifted children—teaching them strategies and the politics of how to challenge the establishment successfully. Why get your head chopped off if you can walk away with change and only a few bruises here and there?

Q. Can you recommend any books for my thirteen-year-old child to read? He is a severe perfectionist and no matter how hard I try to help him "balance" his activities, the "perfectionism" always wins!

A. Yes. There are a couple that I particularly like and have used with my graduate students as well as elementary and middle school children: Thomas Greenspon's *What to Do When Good Isn't Good Enough: The Real Deal on Perfectionism: A Guide for Kids*, and Earl Hipp's *Fighting Invisible Tigers* (1995). Both of these books deal with the possible underlying causes of perfectionism, suggest ways to recover, and offer a sense of humor while doing so.

NOTE

1. Excerpted from *Perfectionism: What's Bad about Being Too Good?* Revised and updated edition by Miriam Adderholdt and Jan Goldberg © 1999. Used with permission from Free Spirit Publishing, Inc., Minneapolis, MN, 1-800-735-7323, www.freespirit.com. All rights reserved.

Chapter Four

Time Management, Homework Issues, and School-Related Studies (SRS)

I have seen the "misuse" of homework become a crushing negative to hundreds of thousands of all ability level students over my forty-two-year educational career.

For example, Frank's Math I teacher would sometimes assign nightly homework of up to 105 problems. First, if Frank already understood the classwork, then wouldn't five or six similar problems be enough reinforcement? And if he didn't get the day's lesson, where was the teacher in the evening to help with the comprehension and solutions?

The time alone needed to solve 105 math problems is a crusher for many students, not to mention the time needed to complete other teacher assignments accumulated throughout the day.

I believe homework is the number one enemy of gifted children and perhaps all children in our American schools. The entire use of, or rather misuse of, homework continues to frustrate me as an educator and a parent. If I started listing the horror stories I've seen and heard concerning homework over the years of my career, I still wouldn't be finished writing this book twenty years from now. There are clear-cut answers to avoid this often negative and counterproductive pitfall in the misuse of homework, which I deal with throughout this chapter. Keep reading.

Q. My child has been identified as "gifted," yet the only difference I can see in her school is "more" and "harder" homework. This doesn't seem right to me. Do you agree?

A. Yes, I agree. This is not right. The three classic misuses of gifted children in our educational system are:

1. Use of high-achieving students as tutors for the slower-achieving students,
2. Piling on more enrichment activities at grade-level expectations to keep the gifted students learning or occupied while their slower-achieving classmates work on completing their own assignments, and
3. Assigning more and harder work to the gifted students; in effect, this becomes a punishment for being bright.

A great deal of this problem can be eliminated through the use of curriculum compacting, subject integration, and curriculum differentiation. Pretesting and posttesting the achievement levels of the gifted student before teaching and then compacting can save weeks and months of repetitive work. Prescribing appropriate work at their aptitude and achievement levels is a clear key in the education of our gifted children in America. You need to talk with your daughter's teacher(s) now, if not sooner!

Figure 4.1.   What are you doing?

Q. Our eight-year-old daughter seems to possess quite a talent on the violin and has been playing/studying with a local violinist in the philharmonic since she was five. Her teacher feels JoEllen has a very promising career. Just one problem . . . all she wants to do is practice the violin to the exclusion of all her other school assignments! We continue to receive notes from her teacher(s) about incomplete and/or assignments never done. What are we to do? The word "prodigy" has been used in reference to JoEllen.

A. If there is such a thing as a good dilemma, then I believe you have one. This is where your job as a parent begins. JoEllen is unique and uniquely talented:

1. Meet with your school personnel and discuss ways JoEllen's schooling/assignments might be modified to support her musical genius.
2. Set up a time management sheet for daily, short-term, and long-term assignments with your daughter. I've included a sample at the end of this chapter. Her learning style may be "abstract random," which could make it more difficult for her to focus on a multitude of assignments and manage her time wisely. This is not an uncommon problem.
3. Set aside an agreed amount of time at home after school where JoEllen can work on specific assignments or school-related studies in a quiet, personal space. This will help her focus and reinforce responsibility. The same can be true for violin practicing time and family interactions, such as dinner together.
4. Check to see if the amount of "homework" being given to your fourth grader is fair and/or necessary.
5. Communicate with your daughter regularly. Many gifted children have a great need to talk. This helps them sort out issues and not make mountains out of molehills.
6. Repeat #1 on a regular basis.

Q. In primary school, our eight-year-old son tested off the charts in both math and reading. What should we do to ensure he receives an appropriate education for his achievement level?

A. When I was the facilitator for gifted and talented K–8, I was assigned to a gifted third grader, who in kindergarten had scored post–high school in aptitude and achievement tests. Frank's greatest cognitive gift is in the field of mathematics. He is quite brilliant in this academic arena. Yet his homeroom teacher insisted that he should "clean and organize" his desk like everyone else. . . that he shouldn't receive any special privileges. Here we had an eight-year-old whose mathematical aptitude surpassed his peers by at least nine years, if not more. His brain was working at a level beyond most of us, yet

Figure 4.2. Perfectionism.

keeping his desk in order was one of the priorities of Frank's teacher. This simply was not an easy task for this child—and quite frankly, probably was not a priority in his brain.

I used to go into his classroom twice a week about two hours after the school-children and teacher had gone home and clean/organize Frank's desk for him. You see, I believed this was one of many small ways I could help Frank.

I also met with him weekly, developed a social/emotional trust, and worked on issues of perfectionism, and we became respected friends. These were many large ways I knew could help him.

I must compliment Frank's school and district in general for developing and adapting a program to educationally serve his cognitive giftedness and social development.

As a second grader, Frank spent forty-five minutes a day in a sixth-grade mathematics class. While trying to close the gap academically, this was an uncomfortable situation socially for Frank—quite understandable. In third grade, the sixth-grade math teacher voluntarily gave up her daily planning time four days a week and was paid tutoring time by the district to work with Frank on mathematics.

As a fourth grader, his parent(s) drove him to the middle school, where Frank took Math I first period with eighth and ninth graders. He scored a scaled score of 96, a Level 4 on the New York State Regents. And on the successful story goes . . . a scaled score of 100, a Level 4 on Math II Regents. Frank was on the TV special *America's Genius: Level II*, where he made it through to the semifinal round, winning a $25,000 college trust fund, a trip for four to Hawaii, a 68" color TV, a Palm Computer, and an all-expenses-paid trip for himself and his family to and from Los Angeles.

I've mentioned all this to you because JoEllen and Frank are unique, prodigies if you will. Frank did not clean and organize his desk. JoEllen does not always complete assignments. As parents and educators we can help these and other children manage time, set priorities, and achieve a balanced and healthy life for themselves.

We can also work with our children's schools to help in the development of their appropriate and adequate education. There are models that do exist.

Frank graduated as valedictorian of his high school senior class in the Webster Central School District in 2006. As he concluded his speech at commencement, all 493 of Frank's peers gave him a roaring standing ovation. I had happy tears in my eyes as the audience of parents stood too.

Bravo, Frank.

Following is his valedictorian speech for you to enjoy:

Good afternoon, Mr. Strining, the Board of Education, Mr. Pustulka, Mr. Koeng, faculty and staff, family and friends, and the class of 2006. In a few moments, we'll all be walking across the proverbial (and literal) stage. It's quite an event; it's the culmination of thirteen years of Webster-sponsored education and oppression. Remember being forced to walk around in single-file lines? Or those lovely agendas that they yelled at everyone for not carrying? And that amazing Senior Project. That was fun. But first, because the school said so, I get to say some crazy things that probably nobody cares about. I hope, however, that this will be reasonably painless, and maybe even interesting.

I'll start with a story. Stories are great. They can be funny, interesting, inspirational, and all that other great stuff. According to AP Lit, they can be interpreted in many weird and twisted ways. This premium story is about a certain chicken named Mike. Mike was a pretty ordinary chicken, except he didn't have a head. Normally, when we think about headless chickens, we think about those big freezers that they have at the supermarket. And that could have been Mike's fate. Mike wasn't always headless; in fact, for the first five and a half months of his life, he had a perfectly functional head. Then, one day, his owners decided that they wanted to have some chicken. They were hungry, and they knew that their bellies weren't going to fill themselves. Plus, chicken was, and still is, a tasty treat. So, the owner went out back, put Mike's neck on a block, and severed it with an axe. What happened next was amazing. Instead of dying, as one would normally expect a chicken to do in such a situation, Mike decided to walk around. "Running around like a chicken with its head cut off" is not an uncommon expression. Maybe it's a good way to describe how everyone will be acting after this ceremony. But most people probably don't think about Mike.

Mike's behavior really wasn't as chaotic as one would expect it to be. It was quite similar to his predecapitation behavior; he tried to crow and even peck for food as if he still had a head. Obviously, he wasn't terribly successful at either activity, but he still tried. Mike was able to survive for another eighteen months, or over three-quarters of his life, without a head. He became a national celebrity, appearing in several magazines. He also spawned numerous copycat creations, and today, in his hometown of Fruita, Colorado, there is an annual festival in his honor.

The point of that story isn't simply to gross everyone out. There is actually an important moral to the story. A terrible misfortune for Mike became a unique opportunity. He was able to live much longer than he was supposed to, and he became far more famous than he could have been had he not lost his head. According to such famous personalities as John F. Kennedy and Lisa Simpson, the Chinese term for crisis contains the character that represents opportunity. This isn't actually true; it would be quite a stretch to interpret the character as "opportunity." But people don't start these myths just for fun; they do so to spread important ideas.

Of course, we don't have to be chickens, nor must we lose our heads, to appreciate this wisdom. In fact, if it weren't for a certain misfortune that I faced, I probably wouldn't have a speech today. A couple weeks ago, my beloved Rubik's Cube broke, and I wasn't able to fix it. This dramatically reduced the amount of time that I wasted by playing with the cube, and I had more time to write this speech. And then there was the time I got rejected by my first choice college. It had been my dream school for thirteen years, so obviously I was quite disappointed. However, the rejection gave me the opportunity to explore other colleges that I wouldn't have considered, ones that I later decided were probably better for me.

Everyone knows that commencement is a major transition, to a new environment, and a new life. As we leave high school, with its micromanaged schedules and tightly controlled bathroom breaks, and enter our new lives, we will encounter new kinds of misfortunes and crises, like failing a course, not getting that promotion, or even losing a job. In any troubling situation, however, it is important to remain optimistic and to look for opportunity, as Mike did. So, if you ever have problems with that differential equations course, or if your car breaks down four times in a week, remember what Oscar Wilde said: "What seems to us as bitter trials are often blessings in disguise."

Q. What's the proper amount of after-school and weekend activities I should have my child involved in?

A. Many gifted children are multipotential. They have the ability and desire to do unlimited amounts of cognitive, social, and athletic activities. In theory, this is wonderful! In practice, it can be less than a positive.

I've always been a huge proponent for creative thinking and emotional/physical relaxation. I would occasionally give only one "homework assignment" for an evening to my elementary and middle school students. This was in my pre–"school-related studies" (SRS) days. It would be to go to their bedrooms for thirty minutes, shut their doors, and lie down on their beds and relax.

Their initial reactions were almost comical. "Dr. C, what do you want us to do while we lie there? What should we think about? What if we fall asleep? Can I read? Can I talk to my friend(s) on the phone? What if I can't stay in one place that long?"

To me, these questions were a clear indication that our children are overextended—and more important, they haven't been taught and/or slowed down enough to think for themselves and relax.

I simply responded by saying, "Your only assignment is to go in your bedroom for thirty minutes, shut the door, and lie down on your bed. Cover up with a cozy blanket if you want."

Regardless of the grade or age level I tried this with, the results were almost uniform.

Some children slept for well more than a half-hour. Others thought about their friends and family relationships—good features, as well as areas that needed improvement(s).

Still others read—a book they personally enjoyed rather than an assigned book or a specified amount of pages/chapters. One sixth grader read for five hours and "polished off" the Newbery book *Maniac Magee*. Wow, what a concept—reading for pleasure—an art form we're losing because we are overloading our children with preassigned homework and assigned readings every day and weekend.

When we'd have a school holiday, I'd ask the children to take just one hour of that day and pick an SRS activity of their choice. I told them I would do the same.

Bedrooms were organized, students caught up on assignments, a majority read books of their choice, while others developed their own web pages or worked on the computer.

My overriding suggestion to you is to make sure your child has time during the week to reflect, rest, do assignments, catch up on assignments, eat dinner with the family, talk, and not be out of the house every afternoon and/or night.

You'll definitely know your child is overinvolved if he or she is cranky, overtired, stressed, not finishing assignments, or doing projects/assignments without quality—instead, racing to get things done.

Balance is such an important concept in our mental, physical, family, social, and academic health. We owe it to our children to help them time manage, select, and achieve balance in their lives.

Q. I'm at my wit's end. My fifteen-year-old gifted child is an extreme procrastinator and consequently, his grades suffer due to assignments turned in late. Can you please help?

A. Yes, I can, and this "homework hazard" is not uncommon for gifted students—and adults! Many of us like to work under "last-minute stress," but this is different from perfectionists who avoid getting started due to fear of failure and procrastination.

You will be an enormous help to your son by sitting down with him and talking through the approximate amounts of time he'll need for his daily, short-term, and long-term assignments. Then make sure he has a quiet place to study and enforce an agreed amount of time for his daily studies at home.

If your son is involved with musical activities, sports, and/or school clubs, you need to think about whether or not he is overextended. There are only so many hours in a day and week, and he needs a balance between work and play.

Q. My son is always leaving his assignments (work) until the very last minute. Then he panics, gets the entire house in an uproar (emotionally and physically), and many times winds up staying up the entire night before the project is due. I'm at my wit's end and don't know how to help. Please advise!

A. You can very definitely help your son by sitting down with him and plotting out on a calendar when his long-term and short-term projects and assignments are due. Then you need to pick a mutually agreeable time with him when he'll do his work at home each day . . . no excuses. Many times, the hardest part of doing a project or assignment is getting started. Having an assigned time to study/work at home each day is the best way to help your child get started and avoid these last-minute panics and family disruptions. I've included an example of a monthly time management calendar here for you.

Figure 4.3.   Procrastination.

TIME MANAGEMENT SHEET

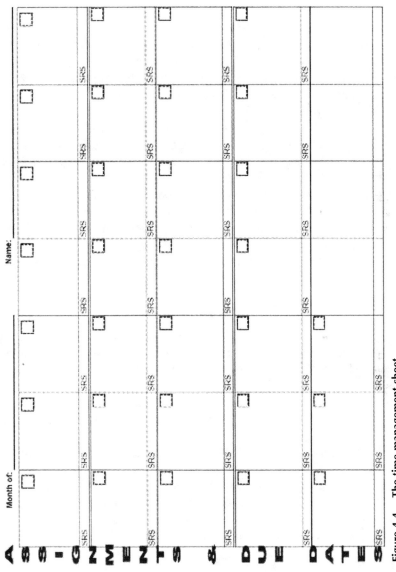

Figure 4.4. The time management sheet.

FIVE TIPS FOR PROCRASTINATORS

1. Plot out your daily, short-term, and long-term assignments on the monthly time management sheet I've included at the end of this chapter. Seeing the actual schedule makes the workload far less intimidating and much easier to tackle.
2. Find a quiet room in your home that you can claim at anytime for your studying purposes. "Try" to keep it organized!
3. Set aside one hour every weekend to clean your bedroom, organize your thoughts, and look over your upcoming assignments for the next week. This helps you focus and calm down!
4. Look over the coming week's TV shows and specials in your local TV Guide. Allow yourself a half-hour or hour a day where you can relax and unwind and catch up on your favorite shows. Looking forward to this treat keeps you motivated on your study tasks.
5. Plan out a tentative time of day, afternoon and/or evening, when you will work on your school assignments and other commitments each day. Discuss this with your parents so they can support you and help other family members (siblings) respect your quiet study time. Be flexible. A large block of time Saturdays (two hours) can help avoid the Sunday evening panic and shortage of time.

SCHOOL-RELATED STUDIES (SRS)

I developed school-related studies (SRS) twenty-five years ago to help students and parents relate learning as an "ongoing" process occurring naturally, linking their school daytime and thinking with their evening at home. Its goal was to reinforce, extend, and enrich learnings presented in school. It has worked equally successfully with first graders, fourth graders, middle schoolers, and every age in between.

For a majority of students the issue of homework had become a negative force rather than the positive educational practice it was originally intended to be—a practice or reinforcement of newly studied objectives. This truly hurt my heart, as learning can be a joyful gift in life. Thus, I invented SRS!

School-related studies are intended to:

- Foster a love of learning in all students
- Promote ongoing learning outside the school setting
- Improve students' independent work habits
- Strengthen the communication between home and school

- Raise standards and improve academic performance
- Address individual interests and needs of students at all academic levels

I expected a minimum designated time period to be maintained after school for school-related studies by all of my students five or six days out of seven each week. Parents agreed to help their children select a quiet, well-lighted area where their child/children could attend to their SRS. They also helped their child/children make good decisions as they related to their choice of activities. This provided a pleasant, cooperative family planning time together.

During SRS students usually prioritize their work as follows:

1. Complete any unfinished classwork or assignments due the very next day if not completed in school-allotted time.
2. Study for upcoming tests, work on long-term projects, and/or review work covered in class.
3. Choose something related to thinking/school topics that supported academic interests/needs. This could include reading a book of choice, visiting the library, organizing their bedroom, writing a thank-you note, visiting a town board meeting for government, studying for Math Olympiads, working on an art project or Odyssey of the Mind project, to mention just a few.

Suggested minimum time arrangement per grade level were as follows:

Table 4.1. Minimum Time Arrangement per Grade Level

Grade	Minutes
Kindergarten	20 minutes
First Grade	25 minutes
Second Grade	30 minutes
Third Grade	35 minutes
Fourth Grade	40 minutes
Fifth Grade	50 minutes (September through December)
Sixth Grade	75 minutes (January through April)
	60 minutes (May and June)

School-related studies definitely empowered parents as prime supporters of their children's focused and daily quiet study times at home. It also helped the children focus on daily and long-term assignments. Gone were the daily adages between parent and child:

"Hi, Johnny. How was your day at school today?"

"OK, Mom."

"Any homework tonight?"

"No, Mom."

Ha! Ha! Home and school become linked with similar and united expectations.

The biggest and most positive change I noticed after the initial transition period into SRS was a significant increase in the amount of pleasure reading my students were doing.

This was true across grade levels. My intermediate students and middle schoolers were polishing off Newbery books and other novels they loved in two or three days. In fact, at least one-third of my students significantly increased their SRS time voluntarily! Indeed, learning and reading were becoming pleasurable again!

The same was true for my primary students. Reading time increased two-, three-, and fourfold.

Of equal importance along with positive increases in "attitude toward learning" with SRS were the increases in test scores and subsequent increases in self-concept of my students. As part of school related studies, I required a minimum of 20 percent of SRS to be used three days in a row to study for an upcoming major test. This helped kids get away from cramming the night before a test, helped keep learning from a last-minute review process, and oftentimes helped parents become involved with their child in studying for tests.

Enjoyment in learning, increasing test scores, increasing positive self-concept, strengthened home-school connection and communication, reading for pleasure, applicable leanings, and more—wow, what more could we ask for in a positive and successful school environment.

Bravo for SRS!

Why "S.R.S."?

 ◆ Addresses individual needs of
   students at all academic levels

 ◆ Help improve students'
   independent work habits

 ◆ Teach students "how to learn"
   by utilizing skills such as time
   management, organization and
   good study habits

Figure 4.5.   Why SRS?

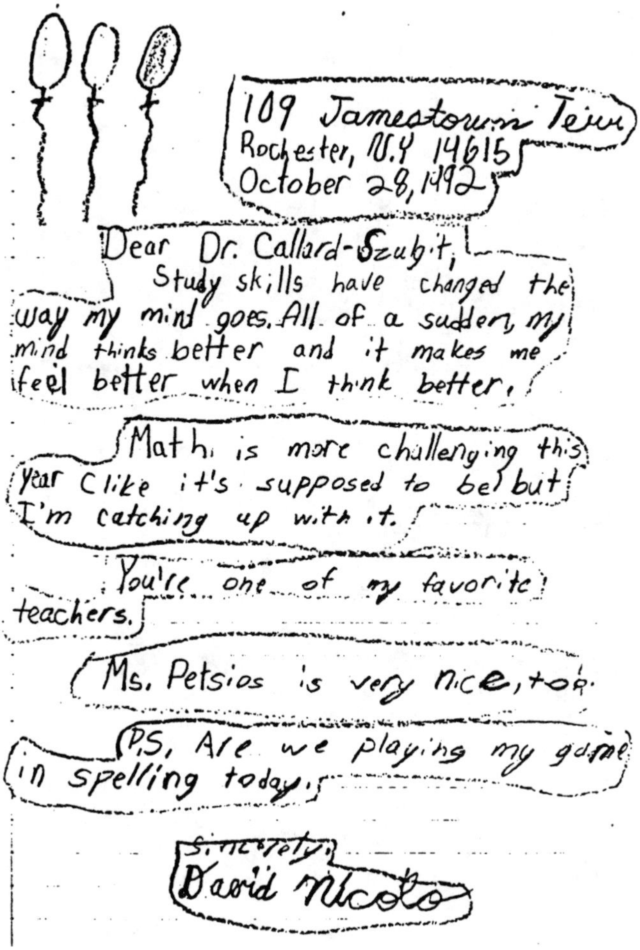

109 Jamestown Terr.
Rochester, N.Y 14615
October 28, 1992

Dear Dr. Callard-Szubit,
Study skills have changed the way my mind goes. All of a sudden, my mind thinks better and it makes me feel better when I think better.

Math is more challenging this year (like it's supposed to be) but I'm catching up with it.

You're one of my favorite teachers.

Ms. Petsios is very nice, too.

P.S. Are we playing my game in spelling today?

Sincerely,
David Nicolo

Figure 4.6. David Nicolo.

649 Old Brook lane
Rochester, N.Y. 14615
October 28, 1992

Dear Dr. Callard-Szulgit,

    I think the study skills program is a great idea! I think it really helps me, because I was always unorganized. Now I'm really organized!

    It really helps me to stay on track with the schedule for the day. I especialy like it because the school related studies helps me get better grades in school.

    I think it is a really great idea to keep someone's mind enriched. I think that you should keep this program going as long as you can.

    My mom really thinks it is wonderful for organization. She always says that she wishes she had some for work.

Sincerely,
Lindsay

Figure 4.7. Lindsay.

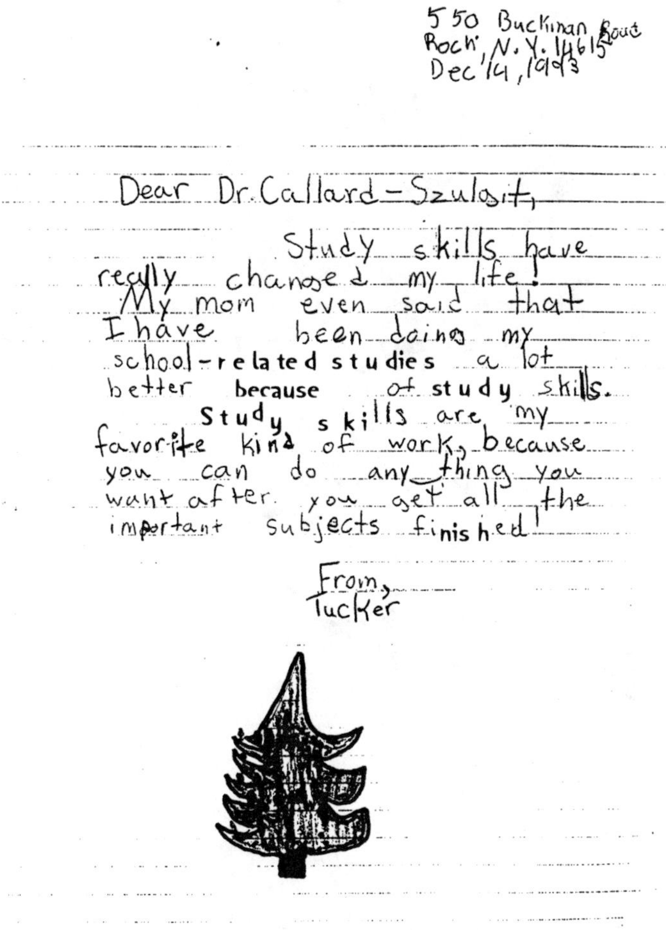

550 Buckman Roud
Roch, N.Y. 14615
Dec 14, 1993

Dear Dr. Callard-Szulgit,

    Study skills have really changed my life! My mom even said that I have been doing my school-related studies a lot better because of study skills.
    Study skills are my favorite kind of work, because you can do any thing you want after you get all the important subjects finished!

From,
Tucker

Figure 4.8.   Tucker.

School Related Studies -

- ◆ *Reinforce*
- ◆ *Extend*
- ◆ *Enrich*

Concepts Presented in Classes

Figure 4.9.   School-related studies.

SCHOOL RELATED STUDIES:

A KEY TO SUCCESS

Figure 4.10.   A key to success.

SQ3R

A time-tested and very successful studying technique is SQ3R, involving the surveying, questioning, reading, reciting, and reviewing of materials. Go over this method with your child and help him or her get into the habit of using it to study.

I used SQ3R regularly with my students and it made an amazing difference in their comprehension and achievement test scores!

Survey:	Look over the entire book, chapter or whatever contents you're going to read. This should include Table of Contents Appendices, Author's Notes, etc.
Question:	Go over the questions at the end of the chapter or devise your own based on what you viewed during your survey. This is especially good for directed reading/study goals and helps keep you focused.
Read:	Begin reading with your questions actively in your mind. When you find an answer, highlight it or make a * nearby.
Recall/Recite:	Try and recite the important information, definitions and answers to questions from the material you just read. If you can, bravo. If not, focus re-read the parts you need to and try again. This is an important step that solidifies the materials in your brain and makes reviewing for tests much easier.
Review:	This can be done in a variety of ways: discussing the material with someone else checking margin notes, highlighted materials and underlined sections, or quickly re-reading. Repeated review helps store knowledge in your long term memory.

Figure 4.11. SQ3R.

Chapter Five

Advocacy

Success is knowing the difference between cornering people and getting them into your corner.

—Bill Copeland

One of my very favorite stories I use in advocacy training, reflecting an educational environment and value system in support (or not) of programming in a school district for gifted is the *Palcuzzi Ploy* (Gallagher and Gallagher, 1994).

Mr. Palcuzzi, principal of the Jefferson Elementary School, got tired of hearing objections to special provisions for gifted children, so he decided to spice up an otherwise mild PTA meeting with *his* proposal for gifted children.

The elements of the Palcuzzi program were as follows:

1. Children should be grouped by ability.
2. Part of the school day should be given over to special instruction.
3. Talented students should be allowed time to share their talents with children of other schools in the area or even of other schools throughout the state. (We will pay the transportation costs.)
4. Children should be advanced according to their talents, rather than their age.
5. These children should have specially trained and highly salaried teachers.

As might be expected, the Palcuzzi program was subjected to a barrage of criticism: "What about the youngsters who aren't able to fit into the special group: won't their egos be damaged?" "How about the special cost; how could you justify transportation costs that would have to be paid by moving a special group of students from one school to another?" "Won't we be endangering the children by having them interact with others who are much more mature?" "Wouldn't the other teachers complain if we gave more money to the instructors of this group?"

After listening for ten or fifteen minutes, Palcuzzi dropped his bomb. He said that he was not describing a *new* program for the intellectually gifted, but a program the school system had been enthusiastically supporting for a number of years—the program for *gifted basketball players*! Palcuzzi took advantage of the silence that followed to review his program again.

The irony this story portrays is that if a school community likes, values, and/or enjoys a program, protests can be nonexistent.

If the community does not value nor support a gifted program, all sorts of protests are voiced! Sad, but true.

Q. What are my rights as a parent of a gifted child?

A. Your rights as a parent of a gifted child are the same as all other parents.

- Your have the right to be your child's number one advocate.
- You have the right to a fair and equitable education for your child.
- You have the right to know when local standardized tests are being given and see sample tests with question and answers.
- You have the right to join your local and state PTA and advocate for the understanding, training, and support of gifted children with programming for the gifted.
- As a member of your school and district PTA, you have the right to expect those organizations to schedule speakers who are experts in the field of gifted education.
- You have the right to know all of your child's test scores and what they mean.
- You have the right to study sessions where differentiated curriculums and classrooms with compacted curriculums are explained to you.
- You have the right to expect your child's teacher to love, respect, and educate your child with the same amount of time and dedication she or he gives to all the other children in the classroom.
- You have the right to feel comfortable and supported by the educational system as a parent and advocate for your child, gifted children, and all children.

Q. How can I be the best advocate possible for my child?

A. Know that as you work in school groups, community organizations, and/ or neighborhood activities, there will most likely be a prejudice against the "gifted." I even found this throughout my career from many of my fellow educators and administrators. Terms such as "elitist" or "egotistical" are often levied in arguments against providing appropriate programs and activities for identified gifted children. Unfortunately, this is often due to a lack of understanding of whom and what we mean by the term "gifted." Many teachers are still not being educated in differentiating and compacting curriculums, which works for all kids—not just gifted. Sadly advocacy for the gifted continues to be unpopular in our society.

Consequently, it's important for you to do your "homework" and familiarize yourself with the definitions and appropriate programming models and curriculum options.

Stay positive as you help other parents and teachers understand this often misunderstood field. Write your local, state, and national political leaders requesting their help in allocating funds and resources for the gifted.

Join your local and state advocacy groups. On the national level, the National Association for Gifted Children (NAGC) provides conferences, publications, and current research about gifted education.

As a stepparent of four gifted children and educator advocate my entire career for the rights of all children, including gifted, I can tell you, advocacy will be a constant uphill journey. I know you can do it! I did! Read on for my suggested steps to follow.

Q. Our daughter, Sally, has an early birthday and could start school this September. This would make her the youngest, or one of the youngest, in her class throughout her thirteen-year school career. She is very precocious and

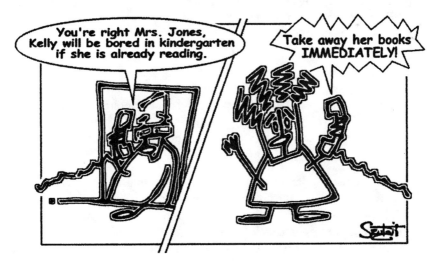

Figure 5.1. Bored if already reading.

started reading at the age of three. I'm torn between starting her in school with all its activities and advantages and knowing she'll always be younger than her classmates. I want to do what's socially, emotionally, and intellectually best for our daughter. What do you suggest?

A. I've done a complete about-face on this very same issue since my career began. In my opinion, all the advantages weigh in on the side of your daughter being one of the oldest rather than one of the youngest in her class. Physically, she'll be more developed; emotionally, she'll have experienced more. She'll have had the advantage intellectually of more environmental influences and cognitive experiences over time.

There are so many games and educational materials available to parents and the general public now. I encourage you to spend quality family time utilizing these with your daughter this next year before entering her into kindergarten. Frequent visits to the public library, overnights with neighborhood children, peaceful times to create and think on her own at home without the pressures of constant homework—she'll never receive these to the same extent again, once Sally starts her public school career.

Another important point to cognitively consider is the extent your school district services its precocious and gifted children. You need to start asking questions and doing some research into the district's policy toward gifted children. If Sally is going to do the same things in kindergarten she already knows how to do at home, by all means, do *not* start her school career early. Take full advantage of that extra year at home.

> The greatest tragedy in education facing today's gifted children is the assumption that they will achieve to their full potential while being instructed at grade level.
>
> —Rosemary Callard-Szulgit, Ed.D.

Q. How are we supposed to know what the "proper" amount of parental discipline is? My husband and I feel very strongly that our children should do their schoolwork, do it well, then "play" all they want. Most of the other parents in our neighborhood are very lax with their children, saying they want their children to have fun and enjoy life! What is fair?

A. Parents are the number one advocates for their children and therefore assume a prominent role in the home setting for rules, expectations for success, and quality of work. They are also role models for peer relationships as well as independent learning outside of work and school.

Creating an atmosphere where your children can be free to develop their own unique and creative talents is essential to their positive mental health. Too much freedom can foster underachievement and an inability to set realistic goals, including time needed to complete short- and long-term assignments.

Many elementary and middle school children need help with time management. As a teacher and parent, I believe it is of the utmost importance for you and your husband to set clear parameters as to when and how much time your children should be spending each day on schoolwork and other responsibilities. Whenever possible, try to have your family eat together. This time provides a wonderful outlet for intellectual thinking, discussions, family closeness, and reflection time with each other.

If your children want "downtime" when they first arrive home from school, I totally support this. Our brains and bodies need peaceful times to relax, reflect, create, and renew—children as well as adults.

From my experience as an educator, I believe there are maximum amounts of time children at various ages should have to spend daily on homework. Please refer to chapter 4. If these times are exceeded on a regular basis, your school's policy on homework needs to be questioned and evaluated.

Discuss and evaluate your rules and study expectations regularly with your children. Include them in the decisions. Compromise can be a very productive win-win situation for you and your children.

You and your husband are the adults in your family with wisdom and experience on your side. Your children count on you to provide a safe and structured home environment for them.

As long as you're fair and realistic, your children will forever be grateful to you for your discipline and caring.

Figure 5.2. Creativity.

Q. We have moved three times during our children's school educations. Both our children, ten and thirteen years old, have been identified as gifted, yet the services provided (or not) from school district to school district vary significantly. How can we meet with our children's current district, asking for an appropriate education and referencing current standards, and not alienate the teachers?

A. I understand your plight, empathizing with you, your children, and your children's teachers. During the past decade, significant numbers of gifted programs have been dropped in districts, some due to budget cuts and others due to the controversy and misunderstandings surrounding gifted programs. The special education inclusion model has been sweeping the country, giving equal access in heterogeneously grouped classrooms to identified special education students and remedial students. A special education teacher "pushes in" to help the regular classroom teacher with the extra classroom numbers, work load, and classroom management, but who is there to help differentiate and cognitively challenge the gifted?

There are some basic steps and information gathering I encourage you to do before the meeting with your children's teachers in your new school district. Please follow the chain of command, starting with your classroom teacher, then include your principal, school counselor, psychologist, G/T coordinator and/or expert when feasible. Always keep in mind you want to work with your child's school personnel, not against! Your do have a voice. Keep it positive, supportive, and pleasant.

- Talk with other parents in your neighborhood, church and athletic club, anywhere you can find them, asking what they particularly like about their children's schooling, including teachers, class sizes, intellectual clubs, community service organizations, fitness programs, and social activities. Of particular interest to you would be the district's attitude/programming service for gifted children.
- Find out if the rights of gifted children and gifted education are protected by law in your state. Currently about 50 percent of the states legally protect the right to an appropriate education for their gifted children.
- Question your children regularly on what they especially enjoy and don't enjoy about school. Are they learning new things or studying lessons and materials they already know? Is a part of every day being used by them to tutor/help slower learning or remedial students? If they finish assignments early, are they required to then go to one of the learning centers in their room or are they given choices?
- Is the curriculum differentiated for them, or are they given more and harder work?

- Have an idea in mind as to what changes/challenges would benefit your children before meeting with their teachers. Change almost always comes slowly, especially in school districts, which are commonly entrenched in a history of rules, bureaucracy, and regulations.
- Always meet with your children's teachers first! Nothing antagonizes a teacher more than being called in by the principal concerning a parent meeting that occurred without him or her. No one enjoys being blindsided—not the teacher, not you, not the administrator, not your children!

Also, a wonderful book has been published as a service from NAGC (National Association for Gifted Children): *Aiming for Excellence: Gifted Program Standards* (Landrum, Callahan, and Shaklee, 2001). It benchmarks standards of excellence in seven critical areas, as follows:

- Program design
- Program administration and management
- Socio-emotional guidance and counseling
- Student identification
- Curriculum and instruction
- Professional development
- Program evaluation

The authors offer an increased understanding of the current standards, providing examples, benefits, outcomes, and possible barriers to the successful implementation of the standards.

I encourage you to read this book carefully and you'll feel and be much better equipped intellectually and emotionally as you approach your children's teachers and administrators.

Q. What is the best style of teacher for gifted children? Strict? Lax? One who requires a great deal of homework? Formal? Structured?

A. You should always expect your child's teacher to have high expectations for excellence, for your child and herself. Of course, this should be true for all children and teachers. Giving large amounts of homework is not a sign of good teaching. In fact, it's just the opposite. If a child already knows how to do the material, such as the current math problems, then doing more than four or five problems at home for review/reinforcement is a sad waste of your child's time. If a child isn't able to do the day's assignment, then sitting in front of a worksheet with thirty problems alone at home isn't going to do him any good, either.

Figure 5.3.   Baby math.

Many times, schools select teachers for their gifted programs who are very dedicated, creative, and caring of their students. That's a start. However, in the past two decades, a multitude of research on teaching gifted and programming for gifted has surfaced. Courses and degrees are being offered at local college and universities in the specialty area of teaching the gifted. At this point, I believe it is not enough to be "well intentioned" as an educator of the gifted. Parents have the right to expect their gifted child's teacher to be credentialed in the topic and continuously undergoing staff development and studies in the area.

I ran a classroom with a great deal of flexibility. If students finished their work ahead of others, they had choices as to what they could do with their time while waiting—read, work on other assignments, do research in the library, work on computer programs, and so on. They still had to check in with me before opting one of their choices. Sometimes I would say, "Fine, just clean and organize your desk, first!"

You should also look for a teacher who integrates spelling and vocabulary lessons from all of the subject areas and special area classes, rather than a premade publisher's spelling books. This makes the vocabulary studies much more applicable.

Differentiating the curriculum and compacting for gifted children make a huge difference in the quality use of their time and optimal learning.

There are teachers who do support the rights of all children, including the gifted. Find them for your child—and find them to give them your support!

Q. How do I find out if my state supports the education of gifted children and what support can I expect to receive?

A. Just a little over half our states have legislation supporting gifted education and even some states without legislation still support this cause. To find out whether your state is proactive and legally involved with education of its gifted, I encourage you to go the website of the Davidson Institute for Talent Development at www.davidsongifted.org.

Q. Once my child has been identified as gifted and recommended for our district's gifted program, must I place Trysta in it? I've heard the homework load is overwhelming for the students who are in the gifted program.

A. I applaud your question and encourage you to talk with the teacher(s) in the gifted program and visit the classroom(s). Seeing and hearing what's going on firsthand is much better than getting information second- or third-hand.

I taught the fourth-grade entrance class for the self-contained gifted program in a district for eighteen years. Parents were often initially overwhelmed at first, by hearing their children labeled as gifted—and second, wondering what the "right" thing was to do for their children.

We would have an introductory evening where our program and philosophies would be explained and discussed. Dozens of questions would be asked and answered. By the end of the three hours, parents walked away with concrete answers based in fact, not gossip.

Having your child labeled as gifted does set him or her apart and doesn't always help. For that reason, I am now a strong proponent of an inclusive process rather than an exclusive program for gifted and all children!

Many parents of my gifted students over the years have become lifelong friends of mine, as have their children. We're all advocating for the same thing—a quality education meeting the cognitive and affective needs of *all* children.

Q. I've had it! I've tried every possible way I know of to get our school district to educate our three children, each of whom have tested five to eight years above the norm in all areas of academic achievement. I even volunteered to help the teachers in the classrooms on a daily basis. The most that has happened is our seven-year-old daughter was given three times more work to do than her classmates were. The same has happened to our two sons! Can I gather support if I pursue the legal system?

A. I must admit, I secretly always hoped that a brave and courageous family would turn to the legal system to help its cognitively gifted children get a fair and appropriate education once our school district had dropped its gifted and talented program. It would also have helped me help them!

There are three sources I would like you to familiarize yourself with before you undertake the legal system for support.

First, find the Jacob K. Javits Gifted and Talented Students Education Act of 1988 . . . Part B. Keep a copy of this with you, and/or memorize the Statement of Purpose (169).

> It is the purpose of this act to provide financial assistance to state and local agencies, institutions of higher education, and other public and private agencies and organizations, to initiate a coordinated program of research, demonstration projects, personnel training, and similar activities designed to build a nationwide capability in elementary and secondary schools to identify and meet the special educational needs of gifted and talented students. It is also the purpose of this act to supplement and make more effective the expenditure of state and local funds and of federal funds made available under Chapter 2 of Title I and Title II of this act, for the education of gifted and talented students.

Simply stated, there have been and continue to be hundreds of thousands of dollars allocated to major colleges, universities, and school districts throughout our country since the inception of the Jacob K. Javits Gifted and Talented Students Education Act of 1988 for the research, demonstration, teacher training, and similar activities related to gifted education. Investigate your local districts to see what funds and programs/projects are available for your children and local educators.

Second is *Gifted Children and the Law: Mediation, Due Process, and Court Cases* (Karnes and Marquardt, 1991). This text is a valuable resource and major contribution in the advocacy of gifted education.

Providing the results of legal action and reinforcing a free and appropriate education for exceptional children (P.L. 94-142: the Education for All Handicapped Children Act), parents can read about cases in which the courts clearly ruled in favor of parents and their gifted children.

Third is *Gifted Children and Legal Issues in Education: Parents' Stories of Hope* (Karnes Marquardt, 1991).

This book is a wonderful resource for parents and teachers who have become exhausted and exasperated in trying to accomplish an appropriate education for their gifted and talented children and students.

Filled with a compilation of personal stories by parents of gifted children, this book lends support to parents by transmitting successfully settled disputes of parents whose determination and fortitude to achieve excellence in education for their own children and all children was victorious!

Q. Our seven-year-old son is reading on a sixth-grade level and is also very verbal. His vocabulary is quite advanced for his age. Paul's teacher is very loving and kind to him, but I'm afraid she is not accommodating his advanced reading skills. I know that IEPs (Individual Education Plans) are developed for identified special education students. Can I request an IEP for my son?

A. I'm afraid many of the states in our country do not accommodate gifted education by law, so requesting an IEP for your gifted child might fall against deaf ears. If your son was identified with special education needs other than gifted, an IEP would be required by law to be developed, adhered to, and regularly evaluated. However, there is a way to be quite proactive in helping your son's teacher develop a plan of reading instruction for his advanced level.

Begin by meeting with Paul's teacher and ask if you both could develop a simple written plan. This could include ideas to be used at school as well as at home.

Second, include the librarian or media specialist in the meeting. I'm sure she or he would be willing to pull sixth-grade reading level materials for Paul that would supplement the texts and curriculum at the first grade. She or he could also develop a list of books for Paul that would be subject appropriate for his age yet written at a higher instructional level.

Third, see if you can involve the school's special education resource room educator. While her job may be defined as supporting identified special education students, perhaps she could fit in twenty minutes two or three times a week to work directly with Paul. I can't imagine there aren't other gifted children in your son's first grade. Small group advanced reading support instruction would be wonderful for the children several times a week if not daily.

Fourth, ask Paul's teacher if she could meet with intermediate teachers in her school and see if they would consider having one or two of their stellar readers meet and read/discuss books with Paul. Perhaps they would invite Paul into their classrooms once or twice a week for reading instruction and discussions.

Fifth, consider volunteering in Paul's classroom to help his teacher. While you're supervising one activity, perhaps she could work directly with Paul and other advanced readers.

There are many opportunities and still more solutions in getting the appropriate reading instruction for your son. By working with his teacher and colleagues, you should meet with some success. Please get all the agreed-upon solutions in writing though and include a time frame in which activities will be completed. Having a written plan helps ensure compliance. Please let me know how this plan works out for you and if you want more ideas, please contact me at szulgit2@aol.com. I'm here to help.

Chapter Six

Gifted Children Talk About . . .

- Being gifted
- Children
- Parents
- Teachers
- School
- Thinking
- America
- A good teacher through the eyes of a gifted child

For years, every summer I ran a two-week cultural arts course for gifted nine-to thirteen-year-olds in our county. The children and I always had a wonderful time together. On the very last morning, I would take a peaceful hour with them—soft lights, easy music—and tell the story of Khalil Gibran's *The Prophet*. I would then ask the children to honor me by being my prophet, answering some of the age-old questions of humankind.

I don't believe I ever underestimated the abilities of my students, but I never ceased to be awed by them.

Following are just a few of the hundreds of responses I received. I'm sure you'll enjoy them as much as the parents and I did.

SPEAK TO ME ABOUT BEING GIFTED . . .

To me, it means something special, something unique. You don't need to get great grades or be very smart. You are gifted if you want to touch the sky, if you want to stretch the limit. If you follow your spirit, your heart, your mind, you are gifted.

Jessica—Age 11

Many people wonder what gifted means. It is my belief that it truly has no specific meaning. It may mean you are talented or smart, or maybe just proud of who you are. You can stretch the limits of this word and make it fit your spirit.

Kat—Age 10

Gifted means being blessed by God with something special.

Steven—Age 12

I think being gifted means having an IQ of 135 or more.

Frank—Age 9

A gifted student is a person who is above the clouds and cannot see the ground from where he started from, but can see his destination in the stars.

Carl—Age 11

SPEAK TO ME ABOUT CHILDREN . . .

Children are like the seeds of the future to me. They are the people who will change the world tomorrow and they will succeed in doing so. They are different from adults in a way that they stretch their hands out to the stars and try new things. They are free at heart, mind, and spirit.

Jessica—Age 11

Children are young adults who have a lot to learn before they grow up.

Eric—Age 10

Children are little people that haven't learned everything about life. They also make more mistakes than adults.

Alex—Age 10

Children are all the members of a particular species that have a mother and father.

Steven—Age 12

Children are people who have very little responsibilities. They can run and play and learn every minute, every instant. They are the plaster, still sifting into the mold, not yet complete.

Molly—Age 10

A child is anybody who is eighteen years old or younger.

Frank—Age 9

Children are very mentally and physically fragile.

Andrew—Age 11

SPEAK TO ME ABOUT PARENTS . . .

Parents are like the sun which nourishes the seed. They love and care for their children, watch them grow and watch them change the world. Parents bring life into the world and raise it. They are the leaders of their children who will be the leaders of theirs. They guide us through the hard times, the times when we don't have faith.

Jessica—Age 11

Parents guide us to our health, our faith, our life. They shape us to be who we are, teach us right from wrong. They are our mothers who brought us onto this earth and the fathers who teach us sports and how to be tough and not to give up. They are our leaders.

Kat—Age 10

Parents are people who try to do the best for their children.

Eric—Age 10

Parents are important people because they help children grow and learn so that they can take their rightful places in the world. Without parents, children wouldn't get the nurturing they need.

Jeffrey—Age 11

Parents are people who can help you when things seem hopeless. Children also reflect their parents.

Andrew—Age 11

Parents are people who shine light on the path of life, even though they cannot walk the whole journey with their children.

Carl—Age 11

Parents are people who gave you birth and boss you around.

Katie—Age 9

SPEAK TO ME ABOUT TEACHERS . . .

Teachers are more than just people who tutor you in math, writing, history, etc. They teach you the precious things which will bond with you for as long as you live. Anyone is a teacher; parents, school teachers, friends, even children. They all help us grow joyously and well. Teachers are filled with love and care. They are friends to their students and all who know them.

Jessica—Age 11

Teachers are people who teach you and help you progress in life; if they are good ones, they will care how you're doing in school.

Andrew—Age 11

SPEAK TO ME ABOUT SCHOOL . . .

School is a building filled with learning. It overflows with children who reach to the sky and succeed. It's where friendship sprouts and people come together into one. When I think of a school, a ring of children holding hands and learning comes to mind. School is a building of courage, trying new things, friendship, and learning.

Jessica—Age 11

School is where people of all ages go to learn new things and be taught the skills that they need in the world.

Jeffrey—Age 11

School can change the lives of millions because it is the place where teachers teach, the children learn, and the cultural world grows.

Molly—Age 10

School is a place where children go to learn things to help them in life. Sometimes people who aren't very good in school don't like school and good students like it better.

Elise—Age 11

School is a place where learning is the key and being with friends is an especially fun part.

Aileen—Age 9

School is a place where average students learn. Gifted students learn anywhere else.

Carl—Age 11

SPEAK TO ME ABOUT THINKING . . .

Thinking is like a seedling which grows through the tangle of my mind. It keeps on flourishing, until it bursts from its shell onto a sheet of paper. Like a waterfall, it keeps on pouring. When a dream forms, I flow with it, wherever it may go. I can travel to the moon if I think about it. Thought is the beginning of a wonderful journey which can take you anywhere in the world.

Jessica—Age 11

Thinking—What is 2+2? If you answered, you were just thinking.

Kat—Age 10

Thinking is when you use your wits to figure out the answer to a problem.

Alex—Age 10

Thinking is when anyone in the world has a thought and studies it in their brain. It is how we come up with ideas that make the world better.

Jeffrey—Age 11

Thinking is what you do when you are trying to figure something out or trying to get an idea.

Julie—Age 10

Thinking is what you do all the time. You have to think about everything you do. You have to think about what question you want to ask me.

Ben—Age 11

AMERICA

My country 'tis of thee . . .
Ringing bells of
freedom unite your
states of
being.
The vastness of your
beauty radiates
Strength and courage
within our
hearts.
Your many cultures
Races,
Religions,
Are a
Rainbow
Projected through
The prism of
Immigration,
Whose artists,
Musicians, and
Scientists,
Make up your nature.

Yet your honorable
Record is not without
Blemishes
Fractures litter your
Surface of bronze,
Paining with the
Violence
Our hates have created.
Americans of different
Color, race or thinking listen
To each other with
Misunderstanding.
Yet the magnificence of your
Freedom dwarfs this and
The other problems
That have survived and grown
Through the decades of striving
For excellence.
Too often your inhabitants
Take for granted the
Fact they have their own
One among many others.
These tones, when played
Together, not only ring true in perfect
Harmony,
But the awesome chorus of our
American Society.
. . . Sweet land of liberty
Of thee I sing.

                                        —Carl Adair

A GOOD TEACHER THROUGH
THE EYES OF A GIFTED CHILD

Acknowledges my uniqueness.
Grants me the opportunities to creatively problem solve.
Opposed to the notion that I must be globally gifted.
Offers enriching opportunities and chances for real-life experiences.

Develops ways for me to learn at my level and pace.
Truly dedicated to my classmates and me.
Eases the tensions with a warm, loving, learning environment.
Appropriately differentiates the curriculum.
Convinced that I don't need to be separated from my peers.
Helps me reach the synthesis level of thinking.
Encourages me to be my best.
Realizes what works for me can work for all of my classmates.

—E'Shantee R. Proctor

PROFESSIONAL ASSOCIATIONS AND ADVOCACY GROUPS FOR GIFTED EDUCATION

American Association for Gifted Children
(Talented Identification Program)
Duke University
1121 West Main Street, Suite 100
Durham, NC 27701
(919) 683-1400

American Mensa, Ltd.
1229 Corporate Drive West
Arlington, TX 76006-6103
www.us.mensa.org

Association for the Gifted Council for Exceptional Children
1920 Association Drive
Reston, VA 22091
(800) 336-3278

Belin-Blank Center
210 Lindquist Center
The University of Iowa
Iowa City, IA 52242-1529
(800) 336-6463 or (319) 335-6148
Fax: (319) 335-5151
E-mail: belinblank@uiowa.edu
www.uiowa.edu/~belintr

Center for Creative Learning
4921 Ringwood Mdws
Sarasota, FL 34235
(914) 342-9928
www.creativelearning.com

Council on Exceptional Children/Eric Clearinghouse on Disabilities and Gifted Education
1110 North Glebe Road
Arlington, VA 22201-5704
(800) 328-0272
www.ericec.org

The Council of State Directors of Programs for Gifted
G/T Programs Consultant
Maine Department of Education and Cultural Services
State House Station #23
Augusta, ME 04333

Davidson Institute for Talent Development, Northwestern University
9665 Gateway Drive, Suite B
Reno, NV 89521
(775) 852-DITD, Fax: (755) 852-2184
www.ditd.org

Gifted Development Center (a service of the Institute for Advanced Development)
Directed by Linda Silverman, Ph.D.
1452 Marion Street
Denver, CO 80218
(303) 837-8378, Fax: (303) 831-7465
www.gifteddevelopment.com

The Hollingworth Center for Highly Gifted Children
www.hollingworth.org

The Institute for Law and Gifted Education
909 South 34th Avenue
Hattiesburg, MS 39402

The Mega Foundation
www.megafoundation.org

National Association for Gifted Children (NAGC)
1707 L Street, N.W.
Suite 550
Washington, DC 20036
(202) 785-4268
Fax: (202) 785-4248
E-Mail: nagc@nagc.org

National Association of State Boards of Education
526 Hall of the States
444 North Capital Street, N.W.
Washington, DC 20001
(202) 624-5845

National Center for Learning Disabilities
381 Park Avenue South, Suite 1401
New York, NY 10016
(212) 545-7510, Fax: (212) 545-9665
www.ld.org

National Research Center on the Gifted and Talented
University of Connecticut
2131 Hillside Road, Unit 3007
(860) 486-4676, Fax: (860) 486-2900
www.ucc.uconn.edu/~wwwgt/...nregt.html

Supporting Emotional Needs of Gifted (SENG)
P.O. Box 6550
Scottsdale, AZ 85261
(773) 528-2113
E-mail: office@sengifted.org
www.sengifted.com

World Council for Gifted and Talented Children, Inc.
c/o The University of Winnipeg
515 Portage Avenue, Winnipeg, Manitoba
Canada R3B 2E9
(204) 789-1421, Fax: (204) 783-1188
E-mail: headquarters@world-gifted.org
www.world-gifted.org

JOURNALS FOR GIFTED EDUCATION

Creative Kids: The National Voice for Kids
Prufrock Press
P.O. Box 8813
Waco, TX 96714-8813
(800) 998-2008, Fax: (800) 240-0333
E-Mail: CK@prufrock.com

Gifted Child Quarterly
1155 15th Street, N.W., Suite 1002
Washington, DC 20005
(202) 785-9268

Gifted Child Today
P.O. Box 8813
Waco, TX 76714
(800) 998-2208

Journal of Advanced Academics
University of Connecticut
2131 Hillside Road
Unit 3007
Storrs, CT 06269-3007
(860) 486-8759, Fax: (860) 486-2900
E-mail: jaa@uconn.edu

Journal for the Education of the Gifted
Prufrock Press
P.O. Box 8813
Waco, TX 76714-8813
(800) 998-2208, Fax: (800) 240-0333
www.prufrock.com/...prufrock_jm_jeg.cfm

Journal for the Education of the Gifted
University of North Carolina Press
P.O. Box 2288
Chapel Hill, NC 27515-2288

Journal for the Education of the Gifted
1920 Association Drive
Reston, VA 22091

Journal for Secondary Gifted Education
Prufrock Press
P.O. Box 8813
Waco, TX 76714-8813
(800) 998-2208, (800) 240-0333
www.prufrock.com/...prufrock_jm_jsge.cfm

NAGC
1707 L. Street, NW—Suite 550
Washington, DC 20036
(202) 785-4268, Fax: (202) 785-4248
E-mail: nagc@nagc.org

Parenting for High Potential
(Quarterly magazine for NAGC members)
www.nagc.org/Publications/...parenting/index.html

Roeper Review
Roeper City and County Schools
P.O. Box 329
Bloomfield Hills, MI 48303-0329
(313) 642-1500
roeperreview.org

Understanding Our Gifted
Open Space Communications
P.O. Box 18268
Boulder, CO 80308
(303) 444-7020, Fax: (303) 545-6505
www.openspacecomm.com/...order.htm

INSTRUCTIONAL MATERIALS AND CURRICULA

Creative Learning Press
P.O. Box 320
Mansfield Center, CT 06250
(888) 518-8004
www.creativelearningpress.com

Creative Publications/Wright Group
(800) 523-2371

www.creativepublications.com
www.growingwithmath.com
www.wrightgroup.com

Critical Thinking Books and Software
P.O. Box 448
Pacific Grove, CA 93950
(800) 458-4849
www.criticalthinking.com

Math-U-See
(888) 854-MATH(6284)
In Canada: (800) 255-6654
www.mathusee.com

Science, Math & Gifted Products
N7513 537th Street
Menomonie, WI 54751
(715) 235-1840
www.smgproducts.com

The Teaching Company
(800) 832-2412
www.teachco.com

Destination ImagiNation
1111 S. Union Avenue
Cherry Hill, NJ 08002
www.Idodi.org/index.php/home

INSTRUCTIONAL PROGRAMS FOR GIFTED CHILDREN

Center for Talent Development
Northwestern University
617 Dartmouth Place
Evanston, IL 60208
(847) 491-3782
www.ctd.northwestern.edu

Concordia Language Villages (immersion foreign language camps)
90 8th St. S
Moorehead, MN 56562
(800) 222-4720
www.cord.edu/dept/civ

Future Problem Solving Program International
2015 Grant Place
Melbourne, FL 32901
(800) 256-1499
www.fpspi.org/index.html

Davidson Institute for Profoundly Gifted
9665 Gateway Drive, Suite B
Reno, NV 89521
(775) 852-3483, Fax: (775) 852-2184
E-mail: info@davidsongifted.org

EPGY (Education Program for Gifted Youth)
Ventura Hall
Stanford University
Stanford, CA 94305-4115
(800) 372-EPGY (3749)
www-epgy.stanford.edu

Independent Study High School
University of Nebraska
P.O. Box 839400
Lincoln, NE 68583-9400
(402) 472-4422
/dcs.unl.edu/ishs

Internet Academy (K–12)
32020 1st Avenue South, #109
Federal Way, WA 98003-5743
(253) 945-2230
iacademy.org

INTERNET SITES

Davidson Institute
The Davidson Institute is a national nonprofit organization dedicated to supporting profoundly gifted students with free services.
www.ditd.org

EPGY—Education Program for Gifted Youth
http://Kanpai.stanford.edu/epgy/

Eric Clearinghouse for Exceptional Children
www.aspensys.com/eric/index.html

Eric Clearinghouse on Disabilities and Gifted Education
(articles on the education of gifted and gifted/LD children)
www.ericec.org
www.eriec.org/digests.html
www.ericec.org/gifted/...gt-diges.html

Family Education Network
familyeducation.com/email/

Gifted Child Information Blog, Prufrock Press
resources.prufrock.com/giftedchildinformation
Blog/tabid/57/Default.aspx

Gifted Development Center
(comprehensive resource site, including articles about testing issues)
www.gifteddevelopment.com

Gifted Kids Speak
www.giftedkidsspeak.com

The Gifted Child Society
www.gifted.org/

The Gifted and Talented (TAG) Resources Home Page
www.eskimo.com/~user/kids.html

GT-Special List
(for families of twice-exceptional children)
www.gtworld.org/gtspecialist.html

Hoagies' Gifted Education
www.hoagiesgifted.com

Institute for the Academic Advancement of Youth Center for Talented Youth
www.jhu.edu:80/~gifted/

Intervention Central: Your Site for Response to Intervention Resources
www.interventioncentral.org/

National Resource Center on the Gifted and Talented (NCR/GT)
www.ucc.ucon.edu:80/~wwwgt/

NWEA—Northwest Evaluation Association
www.nwea.org/

PG-Cybersource at Davidson Institute for Talent Development
Talent Development (online library of articles on the highly gifted)
www.davidsoninstitute.org/pgcybersource.php
www.ditd.org/ (click on pg-cybersource)

The Tag Family Network
www.telport.com/~rKaltwas/tag/

Uniquely Gifted
(twice-exceptional resource site)
www.uniquelygifted.org

Yahoo Resources for Gifted Youth K–12
www.yahoo.com/text/education/K_12/Gifted_Youth

HOMESCHOOLING WEBSITES

Gifted Children and Homeschooling: *An Annotated Bibliography*
www.hollingworth.org/homebib.html

Hoagies' Gifted Education Page
(gifted homeschooling links)
www.hoagiesgifted.org/...home_school.htm

Home Education Magazine
www.home.ed-magazine.com/wlem_HEM.html

Home School Legal Defense Association
www.hslda.org

Links to Summaries of State Home-Schooling Laws:
www.home-ed-magazine.com/HSRSC/...hsrsc_lws.rgs.html

PUBLISHERS OF BOOKS AND PERIODICALS ABOUT GIFTED

DeLeon Publishing
P.O. 461027
Glendale, CO 80246
(303) 331-8725, Fax: (303) 331-1116

Free Spirit Press
217 Fifth Avenue North, Suite 200
Minneapolis, MN 55401-1299
(800) 735-7323
www.freespirt.com

Gifted Education Press
10201 Yuma Court
P.O. Box 1586
Manassas, VA 20108
(703) 369-5017
www.giftededpress.com

Great Potential Press
P.O. Box 5057
Scottsdale, AZ 85261
(602) 954-4200
www.giftedpsychologypress.com

New Moon Publishing
(800) 381-4743
www.newmoon.org

Open Space Communications, Inc.
P.O. Box 18268
Boulder, CO 80308

(800) 494-6178
www.openspacecomm.com

Prufrock Press
P.O. Box 8813
Waco, TX 76714-8813
(800) 998-2208
www.prufrock.com

Rowman & Littlefield Education
5401 Forbes Blvd., Suite 200
Lanham, MD 20706
www.romaneducation.com

TALENT SEARCHES

Duke University TIP (Talent Identification Program)
Box 90747, Durham, NC 27708
(919) 684-3847, Fax: (919) 681-7921
www.tip.duke.edu

Johns Hopkins
Center for Talented Youth (CTY)
3400 North Charles Street
Baltimore, MD 21218
(410) 516-0337
www.jhu.edu/gifted

Northwestern University
Center for Talent Development
617 Dartmouth Place
Evanston, IL 60208
(847) 491-3782
www.ctd.northwestern.edu

University of Denver
Rocky Mountain Talent Search
(303) 871-2983
www.du.edu.education/ces/rmts.html

Appendix

In this appendix, find information on available grants; let them help support your classroom endeavors. Start by going to Google and typing in "grants for teachers." You'll be pleasantly surprised to find thousands of resources. Following are some others.

The American Federation of Teachers (AFT) has a variety of resources at www.aft.org. Click on "tools for teachers" and "funding opportunities" for a list of grants beyond those offered by the AFT itself. You can narrow your search by grade level, subject area, and more.

Log onto www.neafoundation.org for details on available grants from the NEA Foundation, including the Books Across America program that awards $1,000 grants to qualifying public school libraries that serve disadvantaged students.

Check out the grants available at www.toolfactory.com/olympus and read Frances Lamb's winning application at www.toolfactory.com/olympus_contest/contest_winners/olympus_podcast_winners_December_2007.htm.

Toyota Tapestry Grants is a partnership between Toyota and the National Science Teachers Association, offering large and small grants to K–12 science teachers for innovative projects that enhance science education in the school or school district. Go to www.tapestry.nsta.org.

Target traditionally begins accepting applications in August for its annual field trip grants program. In the meantime check out www.target.com/fieldtrips.

Consider these three "online charities": www.donorschoose.org, www.adopt-a-classroom.org, and www.digitalwish.com. Submit a proposal to any of these websites. If they post it online, it could be underwritten by one or more of a growing list of potential donors who have expressed an interest in helping fund worthy classroom projects.

Two sites, www.grantswrangler.com and www.grantsalert.com, carry listings of available grants, including eligibility criteria and deadlines.

On schoolsgrants.org, click on "grant opportunities" for a list of potential funders, including some available only to applicants in the Northeast.

Click on the "My School Grant" icon at www.DiscountSchool Supply.com and scan eight grant categories, including arts and special education. A recent random search for early childhood grants for New York educators returned 152 possibilities.

The National Gardening Association works with a number of sponsoring companies to provide grants to projects that involve students in gardening. Go to www.kidsgardening.org for details.

I wish you well and would love to hear from you if you are awarded a grant (szulgit2@aol.com). We'll be joyful together!

References

Adderholdt, M., and Goldberg J. (1999). *What's Bad About Being Too Good?* Minneapolis: Free Spirit Publishing, Inc.

Anderson, L. W. (Ed), Krathwohl, D. R. (Ed.), Airasian, P. W., Cruikshank, K. A., Mayer, R. E., Pintrich, P. R., Raths, J., and Wittrock, M. C. (2001). *A Taxonomy for Learning, Teaching, and Assessing: A Revision of Bloom's Taxonomy of Educational Objectives* (Complete Edition). New York: Longman.

Bloom, Benjamin, et al. (1984). *Taxonomy of Educational Objectives: Handbook of the Cognitive Domain.* New York: Longman.

Callahan, C., and Tomlinson, C. A. (1996). *Heterogeneity: Inclusion or Delusion? Can We Make Academically Diverse Classrooms Succeed?* Alexandria, VA: Association for Supervision and Curriculum Development.

Chall, J. S., and Conrad, S. S. (1991). *Should Textbooks Challenge Students? The Case for Easier or Harder Textbooks.* New York: Teachers College Press.

Cimochowski, Anna. (1993). *Close in on Social Studies.* New York: Berrent Publication, Inc.

Colangelo, N., Assouline, S., and Gross, M. U. M. (2004). *A Nation Deceived: How Schools Hold Back America's Brightest Students* (Vol. 1–2). Iowa City: University of Iowa, The Connie Belin and Jacqueline N. Blank International Center for Gifted Education and Talent Development. (Visit www.nationadeceived. org for a free download of "A Nation Deceived.")

Coleman, R., and Gallagher, J. (1995). "Appropriate Differentiated Services: Guides for Best Practices in the Education of Gifted Children." *Gifted Child Today* 18(5): 32–33.

Conrad, Steven, and Flegler, Daniel. (1993). *Math Contest: Grade 7 and 8 and Algebra Course 1.* Tenafly, NJ: Math League Press.

Cymerman, S., and Modest, D. (1984). *SAGE: The Spice of Learning for Gifted and Talented.* Longmont, CO: Sopris West, Inc.

Dunn, R., and Dunn, K. (1993). *Teaching Elementary Students through their Individual Learning Style: Practical Approaches for Grades 3-6.* Boston: Allyn & Bacon.

Erikson, H. (1998). *Concept-Based Curriculum and Instruction: Teaching Beyond the Facts*. Thousand Oaks, CA: Corwin.

Fiedler, E. D., Lange, R. E., and Winebrenner, S. (1993). In search of reality: Unraveling the myths about tracking, ability grouping, and the gifted. *Roper Review* (16), 4–7.

Flanders, J. R. (1987). "How Much of the Content in Mathematics Textbooks is New?" *Arithmetic Teacher* 35(1): 18–23.

Galbraith, Judy. (1983). *The Gifted Kids Survival Guide (For Ages 10–18)*. Minneapolis: Free Spirit Publishing, Inc.

Galbraith, J., and Delisle, J. (1996). *The Gifted Kids' Survival Guide: A Teen Handbook*. Minneapolis: Free Spirit Publishing, Inc.

Gallagher, J., and Gallagher, S. (1994). *Teaching the Gifted Child*. (4th ed.). Boston: Allyn and Bacon.

Gardner, H. (1993). *Multiple Intelligences: The Theory in Practice*. New York: Basic Books.

Gardner, Howard. (1999). *Intelligence Reframed: Multiple Intelligence for the Twenty-first Century*. New York: Basic Books.

Greenspon, Thomas (2007). *What to Do When Good Isn't Good Enough: The Real Deal on Perfectionism: A Guide for Kids*. Minneapolis, MN: Free Spirit Publications.

Hess, L. (1994). "Life, Liberty and the Pursuit of Perfection." *Gifted Child Today* (May/June): 28–31.

Hipp, Earl. (1995). *Fighting Invisible Tigers*. Minneapolis: Free Spirit Publishing, Inc.

IB Learner Profile Booklet. Ibo.org. November 2008.

Karnes, Frances, and Marquardt, Ronald. (1991). *Gifted Children and the Law*. Dayton: Ohio Psychology Press.

———. (1991). *Gifted Children and Legal Issues in Education*. Dayton: Ohio Psychology Press.

Kerr, B. (1996). *Smart Girls: A New Psychology of Girls, Women and Giftedness*. Scottsdale, AZ: Great Potential Press, Inc.

Kerr, B. and Cohn, S. (2001). *Smart Boys: Talent, Manhood, and the Search for Meaning*. Scottsdale, AZ: Great Potential Press, Inc.

Kerr, B. A. (1991). *A Handbook for Counseling the Gifted and Talented*. Alexandria, VA: American Counseling Association.

Khatena, J. (1982). *Educational Psychology of the Gifted*. New York: Wiley.

Landrum, M., Callahan, C., and Shaklee, B. (2001). *Aiming for Excellence: Gifted Program Standards*. Waco, TX: Prufrock Press.

Lenchak. F. R., and Reis, S. M. (2002) Gifted students with learning disabilities. In M. Neihart, S. M. Reis, N. Robinson, and S. Moon (Eds.), *The Social and Emotional Development of Gifted Children* (pp. 177–92). Waco, TX: Prufrock Press.

Piechowski, M. (2006). *Mellow out, they say. If I only could: Intensities and Sensitivities of the Young and Bright*. Madison, WI: Yunasa Books.

Reis, S., Burns, D., and Renzulli, J. (1992). *Curriculum Compacting: The Complete Guide to Modifying the Regular Curriculum for High-Ability Students*. Mansfield Center, CT: Creative Learning Press, Inc.

Reis, S. M. (1994). "How Schools Are Shortchanging the Gifted." *Technology Review* 97(3): 38–45.

———. (1995). "Providing Equity for All: Meeting the Needs of High Ability Students." In *Beyond Tracking: Finding Success in Inclusive Schools,* edited by Harbison Dod and Jane A. Page, 119–131. Bloomington, IN: Phi Delta Kappa.

Reis, S. M., Westberg, J., Kulikowich, J., Caillard, F., Hebert, T., Purcell, J. H., Rogers, J., Swist, J., and Plucker, J. (1992). *An Analysis of Curriculum Compacting on Classroom Practices: Technical Report.* Storrs, CT: National Research Center on the Gifted and Talented.

Robinson, Ann (2006). *Best Practices in Gifted Education: An Evidence-Based Guide.* Waco, TX: Prufrock Press.

Robinson, A. (1990). "Point-Counterpoint: Cooperation or Exploitation? The Argument against Cooperative Learning for Talented Students." *Journal for the Education of the Gifted* 14: 9–27.

Rogers, K. B. (2004). "The Academic Effects of Acceleration." In N. Colangelo, S. Assouline, and M. U. M. Gross (Eds.), *A Nation Deceived: How Schools Hold Back America's Brightest Students* (vol. 2, 47–57). Iowa City: University of Iowa, The Connie Belin and Jacquline N. Blank International Center for Gifted Education and Talent Development.

Ross, P. (Ed.). (1993). *National Excellence: A Case for Developing America's Talent.* Washington, DC: U.S. Department of Education.

Schwartz, L. L. (1994). "Educating the Gifted to the Gifted: A National Resource." In *Why Give "Gifts" to the Gifted: Investing in a National Resource*, 1–7. Thousand Oaks, CA: Corwin Press.

Silverman, Linda. (2002). *Upside-Down Brilliance: The Visual-Spatial Leaner.* Denver, CO: DeLeon Publishing, Inc.

Sisk, Dorothy. (2009). "Making Great Kids Greater: Easing the Burden of Being Gifted." Thousand Oaks, CA: Corwin Press.

Southern, W. T., and Jones, E. D. (2004). "Types of Acceleration: Dimensions and Issues." In N. Colangelo, S. Assouline, and M. U. M. Gross (Eds.), *A Nation Deceived: How Schools Hold Back America's Brightest Students* (vol. 2, 5–12). Iowa City: University of Iowa. The Connie Belin and Jacqueline N. Blank International Center for Gifted Education and Talent Development

Sternberg, R. (1997). "What Does it Mean to Be Smart?" *Educational Leadership* 54(6): 20–24.

Tannenbaum, A. J. (1986). "The Enrichment Matrix Model." In J. S. Renzulli (Ed.), *Systems and Models for Developing Programs for the Gifted and Talented*, 126–52. Mansfield Center, CT: Creative Learning Press.

Terman, L. M. (1947). *Mental and Physical Traits of a Thousand Gifted Children. Genetic Studies of Genius,* Vol. 1. Stanford, CA: Stanford University Press.

Tomlinson, Carol. (1999). *The Differentiated Classroom: Responding to the Needs of All Learners.* Alexandria, VA: ASCD.

Treffinger, D. J., Callahan, C., and Baughn, V. L. (1991). "Research on Enrichment Efforts in Gifted Education." In M. C. Wang, M. C. Reynolds, and H. J. Walberg

(Eds.), *Handbook of Special Education: Research and Practice: Vol. 4. Emerging Programs*, 37–55. Oxford: Pergamon Press.

Treffinger, D. J., Isaksn, S. G., and Dorval, K. G. (2006). *Creative Problem Solving: An Introduction*, 4th edition. Waco, TX: Prufrock Press.

Usiskin, Z. (1987). "Why Elementary Algebra Can, Should and Must Be an Eighth-Grade Course for Average Students." *Mathematics Teacher* 80(6): 428–38.

Webb, James T. (1982). *Guiding the Gifted Child*. Dayton: Ohio Psychology Publishing Company.

Winebrenner, S. (1992). *Teaching Gifted Kids in the Regular Classroom*. Minneapolis: Free Spirit Press.

Winner, E. (1996). *Gifted Children: Myths and Realities*. New York: Basic Books.

Index

About the Author

Dr. Rosemary Callard-Szulgit has devoted her forty-plus-year career to the fair and equitable treatment of all children. She is the current field coordinator for gifted studies in the graduate online gifted certification program at the University at Buffalo (UB) as well as adjunct professor at UB.

Rosemary directs the consulting firm of Partners-for-Excellence in Rochester, New York (www.partners-for-excellence.com) and consults both nationally and internationally with gifted children, their parents, and school districts.

Callard-Szulgit's initial training and teaching focus with gifted education has expanded into districtwide integrated programs servicing all children. Her interest and focus on educating children at their aptitude levels have succeeded through the combination of curriculum compacting, differentiation, acceleration, and counseling.

Recognized in *Who's Who Among American Educators*, Rosemary brings decades of research and classroom experience in elementary, middle school, and university settings to her role as staff development trainer of parents, teachers, and children throughout the country.

She has spoken at the First United States/China Conference on Education, Beijing, and presented for the American Creativity Association, National Association for Gifted, World Council on Gifted, West Virginia Annual Reading Conference, and the United States/Russia Conference on Education, as well as consulting throughout the United States.

Dr. Callard-Szulgit continues to have articles and books published dealing with education and parenting of gifted children and has had the privilege of raising four gifted stepchildren with her husband, Karl.

Breinigsville, PA USA
01 July 2010
240990BV00003B/7/P